Get INVOLVED!

Student's Book
with Digital Student's Book

Catherine McBeth   Patricia Reilly

Get INVOLVED!

Collaborative projects

Collaborate with your classmates to develop your problem-solving skills in the WDYT? projects. Become an expert on a topic and get involved with others in your class.

Real-world content

Learn about culture while you learn English. *Get Involved!* is full of real-world content, so go online and learn more about the people, events and places in the book.

Super skills

Get Involved! helps develop your critical thinking, collaboration, creativity and communication skills, which are essential for life in the 21st century.

COLLABORATION **CRITICAL THINKING**

COMMUNICATION **CREATIVITY**

Building skills for the real world

Social and emotional learning

Get Involved! helps you develop strategies to deal with social situations and gives you the vocabulary you need to discuss emotions that you or others experience.

Media-rich content

Get Involved! videos help you with critical thinking, communication and project presentations and improve your video literacy skills.
Access On-the-Go Practice on your phone through the Macmillan Student's App and improve your English with gamified content.

Inclusive classroom

Show your strengths and talents by putting your investigative skills and logic to the test with *Get Involved!* Brain teasers. Learn at your own pace with graded Workbook activities and The longer read.

These creatures sleep in trees, in nests which are made of leaves. In the wild, they're found only in Africa. They're very intelligent – one of these creatures was sent into space in 1961!

Can you guess the animal?

1 ☆ Are the sentences formal or informal?
1 Hi, Jack. How are you? ___informal___
2 I am writing to apply to take part in your show. ___
3 I know you'll love my new product. ___
4 I enclose a photo of my product. ___

2 ☆☆ Complete the formal letter with the phrases in the box.

UNIT	VOCABULARY	GRAMMAR	READING AND CRITICAL THINKING
STARTER What do you know? Page 6	**Vocabulary:** activities, likes and dislikes, adjectives, the environment		
1 Amazing people **WDYT?** Who inspires you? Page 12	Describing people Personal qualities Verb and noun collocations: helping others ▶ Could you work in space?	Past simple, past continuous and *used to* *when* and *while* Subject and object questions	**A magazine article** *Unique strengths* **Subskill:** Reading for gist/skimming
2 Love to learn! **WDYT?** What's the best new skill you've ever learnt, and how can you teach it to others? Page 24	Skills and abilities Learning techniques ▶ Sophie's monthly update	Present perfect with *for*, *since* and *How long …?* *just*, *yet* and *already* Present perfect and past simple	**Online reviews** *Learn new skills!* **Subskill:** Scanning for specific information
3 Look after yourself **WDYT?** How can you improve your health? Page 36	Staying healthy Health and well-being Phrasal verbs: healthy habits ▶ Ethan's top tips	Modal verbs Gerund and infinitive	**An advice page** *Mind what you eat!* **Subskill:** Understanding new words
4 Invention **WDYT?** What makes a good invention? What's the best way to present it to people? Page 48	Jobs in science Verb and noun collocations: science Describing products ▶ The perfect pitch	Past perfect Relative pronouns Defining relative clauses	**An online article** *Science making a difference* **Subskill:** Identifying text purpose
5 Smile! **WDYT?** Who took the first selfie? Page 60	Describing art Photography Types of art and word families ▶ A different kind of portrait	The passive: present and past Active and passive The passive: questions and answers	**An online article** *Smile please!* **Subskill:** Using images and captions to help understand a text
6 Let's go! **WDYT?** How can travel help us to learn about the world? Page 72	Transport Travelling Extreme adjectives ▶ Taking the high road	Future tenses: review Present tenses with future meaning Future continuous	**An interview** *Miro's real world-schooling adventure* **Subskill:** Identifying facts and opinions
7 Choices **WDYT?** Do we control technology or does it control us? Page 84	IT Technology Phrasal verbs: screen–life balance ▶ Question time: technology	First and second conditional Third conditional	**An infographic** *Digital DOs and digital DON'Ts* **Subskill:** Understanding reference words
8 In the news **WDYT?** How do we know if news is reliable? Page 96	Types of media The news Reporting verbs ▶ Fact or fiction?	Reported speech Reported offers, requests, suggestions and commands	**A web page** *How to spot fake news* **Subskill:** Navigating web pages
9 Look what you know! Page 108	**Vocabulary** and **Grammar** review		**Reading:** review of subskills
	Pronunciation p116	Project planner p118	

LISTENING	REAL-WORLD SPEAKING	WRITING	PRONUNCIATION	PROJECT
Grammar: present simple and present continuous, comparative and superlative adjectives, *was/were* and *there was/there were*, quantifiers *too, too much/many, (not) enough, a/an, some/any, much/many, a few, a lot of*, past simple and *used to*				
A radio interview about an inspirational teenager **Subskill:** Predicting what you will hear	Giving an opinion	**A profile** **Subskill:** Using conjunctions – *because, so, although*	*-ed* endings: /d/ /t/ /ɪd/ Silent letters	Create a video about an inspiring person. **Communication** Verbal and non-verbal communication
A podcast about learning languages **Subskill:** Remembering what you hear	Asking for and giving information	**A blog** **Subskill:** Using tenses correctly	Recognising contractions	Create a tutorial to teach your classmates a new skill. **Critical thinking** Finding the best solution for a problem
An informal conversation about healthy habits **Subskill:** Recognising informal speech	Giving instructions	**An informal email** **Subskill:** Using punctuation	Short /ɒ/ and long /ɔː/	Create a diary of a fitness weekend. **Creativity** Evaluating different ideas
A talk about an invention **Subskill:** Listening for the information you need	Checking information Question tags	**A formal letter** **Subskill:** Using formal language	Diphthongs	Present an invention as a product pitch. **Communication** Using language to persuade people
An audio guide **Subskill:** Checking what information you need	Talking about photos	**An online post** **Subskill:** Using *both* and *neither*	Weak forms: /ə/ with *was* /wəz/ and *were* /wə/	Create a timeline about the history of selfies. **Collaboration** Being flexible to reach a common goal
A conversation between two teenagers **Subskill:** Following a conversation	Buying tickets *Will* for spontaneous decisions	**An opinion essay** **Subskill:** Giving opinions	*going to* /gənə/ Syllables and word stress with extreme adverbs and adjectives	Create a map and itinerary for a world-schooling curriculum. **Creativity** Using visuals
A radio phone-in about surviving without your phone **Subskill:** Understanding sentence stress	Giving advice	**A survey report** **Subskill:** Using indefinite pronouns	Sentence stress	Write a questionnaire to find out about screen habits. **Collaboration** Working collaboratively to do a task
A radio news bulletin **Subskill:** Guessing meaning from context	Reacting to news	**A news report** **Subskill:** Editing your writing	Intonation in reported speech	Report a news story in two different ways. **Critical thinking** Assessing the reliability of sources
Listening: review of subskills		**Speaking:** review of Key phrases		**Writing:** review of subskills
Phrasebook p122	Irregular verbs p126			

STARTER What do you know?

Cats or dogs?

Sushi or pizza?

Yoga or mountain biking?

My favourite things
Vocabulary: activities

1 🔊 1 **Match verbs from A to words from B. Then listen and check. Which activities can you see in the pictures?**

A

| do   eat   go   listen to   play   watch |

B

| horror films   mountain biking   pop music |
| sport   sushi   the guitar   to a concert   yoga |

2 💬 **Work in pairs. Look at the pictures again. Ask and answer about your preferences. Use expressions in the box and your own ideas.**

| I'm (not really) a fan of …   I'm (not very) good at … |
| I'm (not really) into …   I'm (not very) keen on … |

> Do you prefer listening to pop or classical music?

> I prefer pop music. I'm into rap and hip-hop.

Listening

3 🔊 2 **Listen to Fatma and Yusuf talking about preferences. Which of the things mentioned can you see in the pictures?**

4 **Listen again and answer the questions.**
1 Who is more active, Fatma or Yusuf?
2 Which football team does Yusuf support?
3 Which animals does Fatma prefer, and why?
4 Which pet is more popular, according to Yusuf?
5 What is the advantage of messaging friends, according to Fatma?
6 Who isn't using social media at the moment, and why?

Grammar: present simple and present continuous

5 **Read the examples. Then answer the questions.**

> She's taking the dog for a walk at the moment.
> She takes the dog for a walk every day.

1 Which tense do we use to talk about habits/regular activities?
2 Which tense do we use to talk about activities that are happening now?
3 How would you change the examples for the subjects *I* and *they*?
4 How would you make the examples negative?

Starter

Pop music or classical?
Horror or comedy films?
Playing sport or watching?

6 Copy and complete the table with the time expressions in the box. Add the time expressions from exercise 5.

> ~~never~~ hardly ever   often   now
> once/twice a week   today

Time expressions	
present simple	present continuous
never	

7 Look at the pairs of pictures again. Using the present simple, present continuous and time expressions, write …

1 Sentences to describe what the people in the pictures are doing.
She is doing yoga in the park.

2 Sentences to say how often you do the activities in the pictures.
I never do yoga.

Grammar: comparative and superlative adjectives

8 Check the meaning of the adjectives in the box. Find …

> active   challenging   cheap   easy
> enjoyable   exciting   happy   noisy
> reliable   slow   stressful

1 the opposite of *expensive*, *sad*, *quick* and *difficult*
2 two adjectives that end in *-ing*
3 adjectives with the suffixes *-able*, *-ful*, *-ive* and *-y*

9 Copy and complete the table with the comparative and superlative form of the adjectives.

	Comparative	Superlative
Short adjectives		
cheap	**1** (…)	the cheapest
2 (…)	happier	the happiest
Long adjectives		
enjoyable	more enjoyable	**3** (…)
challenging	**4** (…)	the most challenging
Irregular adjectives		
good	better	**5** (…)
6 (…)	worse	the worst

10 Write questions with superlative adjectives.

In your opinion, what's …
1 bad / place to live ?
2 interesting / school subject ?
3 good / type of music ?
4 exciting / sport ?
5 good / pet ?

11 💬 Work in pairs. Ask and answer your questions from exercise 10. Use comparative and superlative adjectives and give extra information.

> In your opinion, what's the worst place to live?

> I wouldn't want to live in a small village. It's more boring than living in the city!

Starter

Our changing world
Vocabulary and Reading

Then ... and now

Henderson island Then

Now

Henderson Island is a small island between New Zealand and South America. It hasn't got any inhabitants; it's 114 km from the nearest town on the island of Pitcairn. Jennifer Lavers, an environmental researcher at the University of Tasmania, travelled to Henderson to investigate **1 pollution/throw away**. When she first saw a few photos of the island online, it looked perfect. All the beaches were clean and there wasn't any **2 water/litter**. But Lavers was shocked when she arrived; there was a lot of **3 plastic/containers** everywhere. She estimates that there are about 37 million pieces of plastic on the island.

Tokyo Then

Now

'Mega-cities' are cities with more than 10 million inhabitants; there are currently 47 around the world. The biggest of all is Tokyo, Japan, with more than 38 million residents. When you compare photos of Tokyo from last century and today, the differences are amazing. Then, there weren't many tall buildings, but now there are a lot. The tallest is the 'Tokyo Skytree' at 634 m. Tokyo is famous for its neon signs – there are more than in any other city in the world. The city uses a lot of **4 energy/waste**, and it is trying to produce more **5 water/electricity** from renewable sources like wind and **6 plastic/solar power**.

1 🔊 3 **Check the meaning of the words in the box. Then read the text and choose the correct option for 1–6. Listen and check.**

> electricity   the environment   litter   plant a tree
> plastic   pollution   recycle   save energy
> solar power   throw away   waste water

2 Look at the words in exercise 1 again. Find:
1 one word that can be a noun or a verb
2 one phrasal verb
3 a synonym for rubbish
4 one material
5 one type of energy
6 three actions that are positive for the environment

3 Complete the sentences with information from the text.
1 Henderson Island is between (…) and (…) .
2 Jennifer Lavers works at the (…) .
3 There are about (…) pieces of plastic on the island.
4 A 'mega-city' has got more than (…) inhabitants.
5 There are (…) mega-cities in the world.
6 The Tokyo Skytree is (…) tall.

4 Read the text again and answer the questions. Use short answers.
1 Are there any residents on Henderson Island?
2 Were the beaches polluted in the original photos?
3 Was there a lot of plastic rubbish when Lavers arrived?
4 Are there more than 10 million people in Tokyo?
5 Were there many skyscrapers in Tokyo last century?
6 Are there any mega-cities in your country?

Starter

Grammar: *was/were* and *there was/were*

5 Read the examples. Which forms do we use with singular nouns, plural nouns and uncountable nouns?

> Jennifer Lavers *was* shocked because all the beaches *were* polluted.
> *There weren't* any people on the island, but *there was* litter everywhere.

6 Complete the text with the correct form of *was/were* or *there was/were*. Is Los Angeles a mega-city now?

LA: from small village to movie empire

In 1841, Los Angeles **1** (…) a very small place – **2** (…) only 141 inhabitants! **3** (…) a lot of countryside and **4** (…) many buildings. Most of the residents **5** (…) farmers. But by 1900, the population **6** (…) more than 100,000. By 1920, the film industry **7** (…) very important, and 80% of the world's films **8** (…) made in Hollywood, in Los Angeles. Now, about 4 million people live in the city.

Grammar: quantifiers *a/an, some/any, much/many, a few, a lot of*

7 Read the examples. Which quantifiers do we use in the affirmative, and which in the negative? Which do we use with question forms?

> Henderson Island is *a* small island but it's got *a lot of* pollution.
> How *much* plastic is there?
> How *many* people live on Henderson Island?
> Henderson Island hasn't got *any* inhabitants, but there are *some* residents on Pitcairn Island.
> There isn't *much* to do there!
> She saw *a few* photos online.

Grammar: *too, too much/many, (not) enough*

8 Read the examples and complete the rules with the words in the box.

| adjective   countable   noun   uncountable |

> Can a city be *too* big? It's a problem if there are *too many* people and there aren*'t enough* resources for everyone.

1 We use *too* before a(n) (…).
2 We use *too much* before (…) nouns and *too many* before (…) nouns.
3 We use *(not) enough* before a(n) (…) or after an adjective.

9 Complete the text with *too, too much/many* or *(not) enough*.

> My village definitely isn't **1** (…) big. In my opinion, it isn't big **2** (…)! There aren't enough places for young people to go out. Although my village is quite small, there's **3** (…) traffic because the main road goes right through the centre. So there are **4** (…) cars and lorries but there are **5** (…) buses to take us to town. I wish I lived in the city!

10 Choose the correct option. Are the sentences true or false for you?

1 My town hasn't got **some/any** beaches.
2 People have planted **many/a lot of** trees in my town.
3 There isn't **much/a few** pollution where I live.
4 My town is **a/an** amazing place to live!
5 We can recycle **some/any** plastic containers at my school.
6 There aren't **much/many** students at my school.

Writing

11 Choose A or B and write a paragraph.

A A description of my town: things I like and don't like.
B My nearest city: in the past and now.

9

Starter

Memories

Grammar: past simple

1 Read Sam's memories. What does she miss?

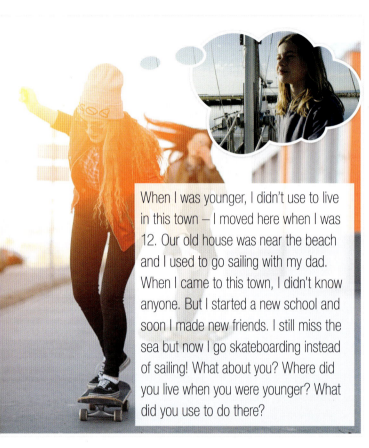

When I was younger, I didn't use to live in this town – I moved here when I was 12. Our old house was near the beach and I used to go sailing with my dad. When I came to this town, I didn't know anyone. But I started a new school and soon I made new friends. I still miss the sea but now I go skateboarding instead of sailing! What about you? Where did you live when you were younger? What did you use to do there?

2 Read the examples and answer the questions.

> We use the past simple to talk about completed actions in the past.
> (+) I moved to this town when I was 12.
> (−) I didn't know anyone.
> (?) Did you live in the same town when you were younger?
> Yes, I did. / No, I didn't.

1 Which verbs are regular and which are irregular?
2 How do we form the negative?
3 How do we form questions?

3 Complete the sentences with the past simple form of the verbs in brackets. Add words or numbers to make the sentences true for you.

1 I (…) **(come)** to this school when I was (…) .
2 I (…) **(not study)** English until the age of (…) .
3 When I was younger I (…) **(like)** (…) .
4 I (…) **(not have)** a mobile phone until I was (…) .
5 I first (…) **(meet)** my classmates in (…) .

Grammar: used to

4 Look at the examples and choose the correct option.

> We use *used to* to talk about past habits or states.
> (+) I used to love sailing with my dad.
> (−) I didn't use to go skateboarding.
> (?) Did you use to live near the sea?
> Yes, I did. / No, I didn't.

1 After *used to*, we use the **infinitive/gerund**.
2 In negatives and question forms, we use **used to**/**use to**.
3 We **use/don't use** *used to* in short answers.

5 Complete the memories with *used to* or *didn't use to* and the verbs in the box.

| call | have | love | not | eat | sing | take |

Embarrassing memories

When I was little I **1** (…) a nickname - my family **2** (…) me Bob because I **3** (…) watching SpongeBob SquarePants. My older sister says that I **4** (…) the theme tune all day long! 😐
— ROBERTO

When I was younger I **5** (…) tomatoes - I couldn't stand them! Sometimes my parents **6** (…) us to Pizza Hut and one day I screamed and screamed because there were tomatoes on my pizza. Now I love tomatoes! 😀
— ESME

6 Write questions with *used to*.

When you were younger,
1 wear / a school uniform ?
2 live / in a different house ?
3 have / a pet ?
4 like / different music ?
5 help / with the housework ?

Speaking

7 💬 Work in pairs. Take turns to ask and answer the questions in exercise 6. Give extra information in your answers.

> When you were younger, did you use to wear a school uniform?

> Yes, I did. I used to wear black trousers and a blue sweatshirt.

> No, I didn't. I could wear anything I wanted.

Starter

What's in this book?

1 Look through your book. Who, what or where are these?

2 Look closer at Unit 1. Match features 1–8 with a–h.

1 WDYT?
2 VIDEO SKILLS
3 CRITICAL THINKING
4 BRAIN TEASER
5 GRAMMAR ROUND-UP
6 Research
7 QUICK REVIEW
8 FINAL REFLECTION

a a section of the unit that summarises all the new grammar and vocabulary
b a section where you watch and think about different kinds of video clips
c an exercise where you practise all the grammar you've learnt so far
d an activity where you have to find out more about something online
e a question that comes at the beginning of every unit, to get you thinking about the topic
f an exercise where you reflect on the process of doing the project
g an exercise that helps you to explore the ideas in the reading text more deeply
h a fun grammar exercise

3 Now explore the rest of the book and answer the questions. Can you answer them all in two minutes?

1 How many units are there in the book?
2 How many pages are there in each unit?
3 What do you always learn first in each unit?
4 Where can you check irregular verbs?
5 How many pages of Phrasebook are there at the end of the book?
6 What can you find on pp4–5?
7 In which unit will you review everything you have learnt?
8 What can you find on pp118–121?

THE CLASSROOM CHALLENGE

4 Match topics a–h with Units 1–8 in this book. Can you be the first to finish?

a scientific developments and technical innovations
b amazing people with unusual abilities
c social media and everyday technology
d art forms including photography and sculpture
e health, nutrition, fitness and well-being
f media, news and fake news
g transport, travel and 'world-schooling'
h learning new skills, from driving and robotics to singing and languages

1 Amazing people

WDYT? (What do you think?)

Who inspires you?

Vocabulary: describing people; personal qualities; helping others; verb and noun collocations

Grammar: past simple and past continuous; *when, while*; subject and object questions

Reading: a magazine article about incredible people

Listening: a radio interview about an inspirational teenager

Speaking: giving an opinion

Writing: a profile

Project: a video – someone who inspires me

Video skills p13

Real-world speaking p19

Project pp22–23

Could you be an astronaut?
In the exciting series *Astronauts: Do you have what it takes?* astronaut Chris Hadfield and a team of experts choose one winner from 12 incredible contestants. The lucky winner gets a recommendation to join the European Space Agency programme.

Now there are only three contestants left, Suzie, Tim and Kerry. Who will win?

Describing people

1 Work in pairs. Look at the adjectives in the box. Use them to describe inspiring characters from TV shows or films. Can you add any more personality adjectives to the list?

| careful   friendly   funny   kind   pleasant   quiet |

> Bart Simpson is very funny.

> I think (…) is friendly.

2 What are the opposites of the adjectives? Copy and complete the table.

Opposites with a negative prefix (*un-*) or negative suffix (*-less*)	Other opposites
kind *unkind*	funny *boring*
careful (…)	quiet (…)
friendly (…)	(…) (…)
pleasant (…)	(…) (…)
(…) (…)	(…) (…)

12

Vocabulary 1

Could you be an astronaut? comments

I expect it will be Suzie or Kerry. Suzie seems **confident** and **reliable**. She's **hard-working** too. Kerry's **enthusiastic** about becoming an astronaut.

Suzie is my favourite. She's **brave** and not afraid to try new things. She's **sensible** – she wouldn't do anything silly.

Tim is intelligent, **calm** in a crisis and **positive** when things go wrong. I imagine he's **generous**, too.

It could be Kerry. She's a **talented** pilot. She seems friendly and **sociable** and **patient**, too.

Tim is **curious** and **creative**. He loves science and new ideas.

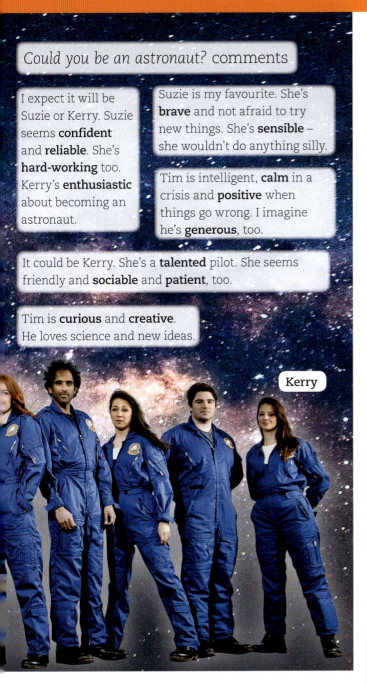

Kerry

Personal qualities

3 Read the introduction to the article and look at the photos. What personal qualities do you think are important for the winner?

4 Read the comments and check the meaning of the words in bold. Who do you think is the best candidate? Why?

5 Complete the definitions with personality adjectives in bold in the text. Then think of someone you know for each adjective.

1 A (…) person can wait for a long time without getting angry or upset.
2 A (…) person gives more of their time and money to others than most people.
3 A (…) person is very interested in learning more about something.
4 A (…) person is very reasonable and practical.
5 A (…) person always puts a lot of effort into their work.
6 You can trust a (…) person to do what they say they will do.
7 A (…) person loves meeting new people.
8 A (…) person is very good at something.
I think the footballer Mo Salah is talented.

6 Write definitions for the other six words.
A confident person believes in his or her own abilities and doesn't feel worried or frightened.

7 Complete the sentences using personality adjectives.
1 I'm (…) but I'm not (…).
2 My best friend is (…).
3 My brother/sister is (…). My mother/father is (…).

8 Work in pairs. Ask and answer about the sentences in exercise 7.

What are you like?

I'm (…) but I'm not (…).

---

to be like, to look like, to like

What **is** Sam **like**? He's generous and confident.
What **does** Sam **look like**? He's tall with brown hair.
What **does** Sam **like**? He likes football and films.

VIDEO SKILLS

9 The video is called 'Could you work in space?'. What do you think you will see? Watch the video and check your answers.

10 Work in pairs. Discuss the questions.
1 What have you learnt from the video?
2 Why do people enter challenge shows?
3 How are challenge shows a good way to learn about a topic?

Pronunciation: silent letters → p116

1 Reading and critical thinking

A magazine article

1 Look at the photos and headline on p15 and answer the questions.
1. Describe the girl. What is she doing?
2. What are the people doing in the other picture?
3. Read the headline. What do you think it means?

▶ **Subskill: Reading for gist/skimming**

Read a text quickly to understand the main message. Titles, headings and content words help you focus on the information that is most useful and relevant.

2 Read the text quickly and choose the best summary.
1. It is an article about how technology can improve people's lives and help them in their careers.
2. It is an article describing how people have recovered from accidents and adapted to change.
3. It is an article that gives information about the powers and abilities people wish they could have.

3 🔊 4 Read and listen to the article. Are the sentences true or false? Correct the false sentences.
1. Chiara has modelled for many years.
2. She learnt to walk again just a month after her accident.
3. Chiara asked a designer to make her a decorative leg.
4. When she was modelling, Chiara hid her prosthetic leg.
5. Orlando had no physical effects from his accident at all.
6. He can calculate what day of the week any day since his accident is.

4 Complete the sentences with the correct name Chiara or Orlando.
1. (…) didn't think he/she would ever do something he/she is doing now.
2. (…) knows things that most people are not able to remember.
3. (…) is able to do something as the result of a change in his/her brain.
4. (…) lost part of his/her body but didn't let that stop him/her doing things.

5 Answer the questions in your own words.
1. What happened when Chiara was coming home from a dance show?
2. When the designer wrote to Chiara, what was she working on?
3. Why is Chiara studying hard?
4. What was Orlando doing when he had his accident?
5. Did Orlando lose his ability after a few years?
6. Does Orlando think he's special now?

6 **Word work** Match the definitions to the words in bold in the article.
1. the job of working as a model
2. occasions when professional photographers take photos for a magazine
3. not willing to let anything stop you from doing something you want to do
4. became healthy again after an illness or accident
5. used for replacing a missing body part
6. a series of actions intended to produce social or political change

7 💬 Work in pairs. Answer the questions.
1. What incredible ability would you like to have? Why?
2. What would like to be able to do better? Why?

CRITICAL THINKING

1. **Understand** Chiara modelled in a campaign for more diversity. Why do people take part in campaigns?
2. **Analyse** What other campaigns do you know about? Think about one campaign and discuss why you think it was successful or unsuccessful.
3. **Create** What problems in society are important to you? Choose one problem and think of three things you could do to make people aware of it.

Research

Find more information about Stephen Wiltshire or someone you choose. What is amazing about them? What would it be like to have their abilities?

Stephen Wiltshire

Unique strengths

We might all dream of being famous, but ordinary people are incredible in so many different ways. We can adapt to new things and learn and grow, as these two interesting people show.

Chiara Bordi is an incredibly positive and confident young person. Chiara did her first **photo shoot** several years ago but before that the idea of **modelling** seemed impossible to her. Chiara was coming home from a dance show when she had a terrible accident. She lost part of her left leg and took nine months to walk again. Then an Italian designer wrote to Chiara – the designer was working on a decorative **prosthetic** leg, covered in crystals. Would Chiara model it? Instead of hiding her prosthetic leg, Chiara made it part of her image. Recently, she did a photo shoot for Models of Diversity, the **campaign** to encourage more diversity in modelling. Chiara is **determined** to focus on what she can do, not what she can't do. Will she become a world-famous model? Perhaps. She's also studying hard, hoping to become a doctor!

Orlando Serrell has got an amazing memory for dates. He's unusual because he didn't have this ability until he was ten. While he was playing baseball with friends one day, the ball hit his head hard. He **recovered** quickly, but had a bad headache for weeks. Then Orlando discovered that he instantly knew what day of the week any date was – but only dates after his accident. Years later, he can still do it. Not only that, but he also knows exactly what he did and what the weather was like on any date since the event! Orlando was surprised when scientists, newspapers and TV shows were all interested in his experience and called him a 'genius'. He thinks he's ordinary.

We can all be amazing humans, whether it's having a talent or skill, working hard to succeed, achieving wonderful things despite difficult circumstances, dedicating your life to helping others or being a good friend. We humans are awesome!

The longer read → Resource centre

Grammar

Past simple, past continuous and *used to*

1 Read the examples and complete the rules.

> Chiara **did** her first photo shoot several years ago.
> Orlando **didn't have** this ability until he **was** ten years old.
> He **wasn't trying** to remember.
> He **could** remember dates.
> Chiara **used to** be a typical teenager, now things are different.
> Orlando **didn't use to** have a special memory.

1 We use the (…) to talk about finished actions or states in the past.
2 We use the (…) to talk about actions in progress at a time in the past.
3 The past simple form of *be* is (…)/*were* and the past simple of *can* is (…).
4 We use (…)/*didn't use to* to talk about past habits and states.

2 Rewrite the sentences in the negative form and the question form.

1 Paul went to the cinema yesterday.
2 I was doing my homework at 9 pm.
3 They were at school yesterday.
4 Lara could swim at the age of four.
5 They used to take the bus to school, now they walk.

3 Choose the correct option. Are the sentences true or false for you?

1 At 3 am, I **slept/was sleeping**.
2 I **went/was going** to the cinema last week.
3 Yesterday, the sun **shone/was shining** all afternoon, so I **went/was going** to the park.
4 I **didn't do/wasn't doing** anything last night. I just relaxed.
5 I **used to live/was living** in a different country, but now I live here.
6 I **arrived/was arriving** at school late this morning. My friends **worked/were working** in class.

4 💬 Complete the questions with *was, were* or *did*. Then ask and answer in pairs.

1 What (…) you doing at nine o'clock last night?
2 What (…) you do after school yesterday?
3 (…) you go anywhere interesting last weekend?
4 When (…) your last birthday?
5 What (…) your friend doing before class started?

when and *while*

5 Read the examples and choose the correct option.

> **While** he was playing baseball, the ball hit his head.
> The ball hit his head **while** he was playing basketball.
> She was coming home **when** she had an accident.
> **When** she got her new leg, she learnt to walk.

1 The **past simple/past continuous** describes a longer background situation or action. The **past simple/past continuous** describes the action or event that interrupted it.
2 We use *when/while* to talk about the point in time something happened in the past.
3 After *when/while* we usually use the past simple. After *when/while* we usually use the past continuous.

6 Complete the text with the correct form of the verb in brackets or one suitable word.

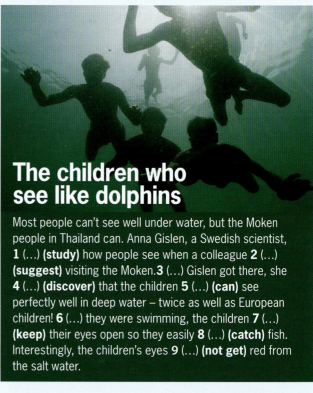

The children who see like dolphins

Most people can't see well under water, but the Moken people in Thailand can. Anna Gislen, a Swedish scientist, **1** (…) **(study)** how people see when a colleague **2** (…) **(suggest)** visiting the Moken. **3** (…) Gislen got there, she **4** (…) **(discover)** that the children **5** (…) **(can)** see perfectly well in deep water – twice as well as European children! **6** (…) they were swimming, the children **7** (…) **(keep)** their eyes open so they easily **8** (…) **(catch)** fish. Interestingly, the children's eyes **9** (…) **(not get)** red from the salt water.

7 Answer the question to solve the Brain teaser.

Romeo and Juliet were lying on the floor – dead! A cat was leaving through the open window and there was water and broken glass on the floor. There was air in the room, but they died because they couldn't breathe.

Can you explain what happened?

Pronunciation: /d/ /t/ /ɪd/ → p116

Vocabulary and Listening

Verb and noun collocations: helping others

1 Look at the text about a radio series. The radio station wants listeners to suggest amazing people. Who would you suggest?

Our world

Do you know someone amazing? **Our world** is doing a radio series on inspiring people – ordinary people who **change society** for the better! Did they **start a campaign** or **sign an online petition** that millions of people signed to help others and change the world? Do they **support other people** to **achieve their goals**? Perhaps they are **helping others** to **gain knowledge**, or **encouraged a friend** to do something, or raised money for a good cause. Whatever it is, we want to know how that person **made a difference**. At the end of the series, one of them will **win an award**! Email or phone us with your suggestions!

✉ inspiringpeople@radio3   📞 0207 365 6987

2 Copy and complete the table with the expressions in red from exercise 1.

Verb + noun	Verb + person
change society	support other people

Collocations
Some verbs and nouns are often used together; this is called collocation. Make a note of examples and record them together. Can you add any other collocations to the verbs above?

win a competition, make a cake …

3 Choose the correct words. Do you agree with the sentences? Why/Why not?
1 People shouldn't win **award/an award** for their work.
2 **Making/Starting** an online petition is a waste of time.
3 Every year you should **achieve/gain** a personal goal.
4 It's important to **change/make** a difference.
5 We should all **encourage/start** our friends.
6 If you study, you gain **knowledge/the knowledge**.

A radio interview

4 Look at the advert for the radio programme and try to guess the answers to the questions.
1 Who is the interview about?
2 What language do they use to communicate?
3 What did Jade win?

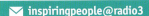

16.30 This week in *Our World*, Daniel Hansen talks about his inspiration, Jade Chapman (right), and her sister Laura. Jade recently won an award for her campaign.

▶ **Subskill: Predicting what you will hear**
Read the questions and exercises before you listen to get an idea of what the listening is about.

5 Read the sentences in exercise 6 and then guess if these sentences are true or false.
1 Jade started the campaign because of someone she knew.
2 Jade's campaign wasn't successful.
3 More people can use sign language now because of Jade's efforts.

6 🔊 5 Listen to the radio programme and order the events.
a Jade won an award.
b Students and teachers at Jade's school did a sign language course.
c Jade wanted to help her sister.
d Jade called her campaign 'Let Sign Shine'.
e Jade appeared on TV and in a national newspaper.
f Thousands of people signed Jade's online petition.

7 Listen again and complete the sentences with a number.
1 There are about (…) deaf people in Britain.
2 Sign language became an official language in (…).
3 (…) % of deaf children and teenagers attend ordinary schools.
4 Jade won a prize of £ (…).
5 The language course lasted (…) weeks.
6 There were (…) places on the sign language course at Jade's old school.

8 💬 Work in pairs. What could you do every day that can make a difference?

> I could join an anti-bullying campaign.

> I could talk to different students in class.

17

1 Grammar

Subject and object questions

1 Look at the examples and complete the rules with *subject* and *object*.

Subject questions
Who inspires you?
Jade Chapman inspires me.
What happened next?
Jade won an award for her work.
Who took the course?
Students and teachers at the school.
Object questions
Who did Jade want to help?
She wanted to help her sister Laura.
What did she do with the money?
She paid for a sign language course at her school.

1 When question words are the (…) of a question, the verb forms are the same as in the affirmative. There are no auxiliary verbs.
2 When question words are the (…) of a question, the verb forms are in the question form.

2 Look at the diagram. Match questions 1–4 with answers a–d. Then write four more questions and their answers.

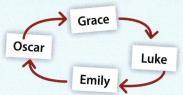

1 Who did Grace help?   a She helped Oscar.
2 Who helped Grace?   b She helped Luke.
3 Who did Emily help?   c Oscar helped her.
4 Who helped Emily?   d Luke helped her.

3 🔊 6 Order the words to make questions about the singer Lorde. Decide if they are subject or object questions. Then listen and answer the questions.

1 happened / after Lorde released her song *Royals* / what / ?
2 encouraged / who / her / to read / ?
3 she / do / what / in 2017 / did / ?
4 who / her / influenced / music style / ?
5 who / she / admire / does / ?
6 what / do / at the MTV Music Awards / did / she / ?

4 Write subject or object questions for the word in bold.
1 I admire the singer **Lorde**. *Who do you …?*
2 **I** admire Lorde. *Who …?*
3 Lorde wrote **the song *Royals***. *What song …?*
4 **Lorde** wrote the song *Royals*. *Who …?*
5 She won **two Grammy awards** for the song. *What …?*
6 Lorde performed with **Khalid** on her international tour. *Who did …? / Who performed …?*

5 Complete the sentences so four are true for you and one is false.
1 Yesterday, (…) texted me.
2 Last night, I phoned (…).
3 Two years ago, I learnt to (…).
4 Last Friday after school I (…).
5 At the weekend, I went (…).

6 💬 Work in pairs. Ask subject and object questions to find out about the information in exercise 5. Then decide which of your partner's sentences is false.

> Who texted you yesterday?
> Who did you phone last night?

7 Choose the correct option.

GRAMMAR ROUND-UP
1 2 3 4 5 6 7 8

Who **1 do you admire/you admire**?
Zoe Saldana! She's very talented.
2 When/While Zoe Saldana was young, she **3 studied/was studying** ballet. Then she **4 decided/was deciding** to become an actor.
What do you know about her career?
She was offered her first film role while she **5 worked/was working** in the TV series *Law and Order*. A few years **6 then/ago**, in 2017, she starred in *Guardians of the Galaxy*.
Who **7 did marry/married** Saldana in 2013?
Marco Perego. They **8 have/are having** three children together.

Real-world speaking 1

ArcelorMittal Orbit Slide

Giving an opinion

1 Look at the photos. What do you think it would be like to go on the slide?

2 🎥 Watch the video. Who enjoyed the experience more – Logan or Mae?

3 Watch again. Then complete the dialogue with the words in the box.

> amazing   brilliant   boring
> disappointing   exciting

Logan
Hi. Did you have a good weekend?

Mae
Yeah, we went on the ArcelorMittal Orbit Slide in London.

Logan
What did you think? Did you enjoy it?

Mae
Wow! It was **1** (…). Totally awesome.

Logan
Really? I went there last month and I reckon it was a bad time to go – it was very crowded.

Mae
Oh, I thought it was a really **2** (…) experience.

Logan
Well, we waited at the bottom for ages, and then it was over so quickly. If you ask me, it was **3** (…).

Mae
But didn't you think the views from the top were incredible?

Logan
Yes, the views were **4** (…). Did you enjoy the ride down the slide?

Mae
I thought it might be **5** (…) but it was the best bit in my opinion.

Logan
I don't know what it was like – I had my eyes shut! It was so fast.

Mae
Oh, I really loved it!

4 Read the Key phrases. Which are in the dialogue?

5 Create your own dialogue. Follow the steps in the Skills boost.

SKILLS BOOST

THINK
Choose a place you visited or an experience you had and make notes about it.

PREPARE
Prepare a dialogue. Remember to include phrases for asking for and giving opinions, and opinion adjectives.

PRACTISE
Practise your dialogue.

PERFORM
Act out your dialogue for the class.

6 **Peer review** Listen to your classmates. Answer the questions.
1 Which place or experience do they talk about?
2 Which Key phrases do they use?
3 Could they improve their dialogue? How?

Key phrases

Asking for and giving opinions:
What do/did you think (of …)?
Don't/Didn't you think that …?
What do you reckon?
I reckon (that) … / I think/thought … / I (really) feel/felt that …
In my opinion …
If you ask me …

Opinion adjectives: amazing, awesome, awful, boring, brilliant, cool, fantastic, incredible, terrible

Real-world grammar

We waited for ages.   It was brilliant!
Did you enjoy it?   The views were amazing.

Phrasebook → p122   19

1 Writing

Soap for health
by Josh Banks

1. Samir Lakhani is a young American social entrepreneur and he works hard to help people in developing countries to be healthier and have better lives. He wants to make a difference.

2. When he was a student, Samir volunteered in a village in Cambodia. He saw that many children got diseases **because** their families were too poor to buy soap. While he was staying in a hotel, he came up with a solution. Guests at the hotel used the soap once or twice and then it went in the bin. Recycling the soap could save lives and be good for the environment! Lakhani started a non-profit organisation called Eco-Soap Bank. Today it has four recycling centres in Cambodia and employs 35 local women. The organisation plans to expand to seven more countries. It gives hygiene-education classes and soap to thousands of people every year. So far, it has provided hygiene education and soap to over 650,000 people.

3. Samir hasn't stopped there. He supports his staff and provides English classes and business skills **so** they can improve their education. He is also developing solar lighting projects in Cambodia, Nepal and Bangladesh. In addition, he has worked on nutrition projects in Cambodia to help people eat more healthily.

4. I admire Samir for many reasons. I think he is generous, enthusiastic and creative. **Although** he is only in his twenties, he is achieving a lot. In my opinion, he is a talented individual and he shows that anyone can change the world.

A profile

1 Read the profile and look at the photos. Why did Samir start Eco-Soap Bank?

2 Read the profile again and match paragraphs 1–4 to the descriptions a–d.
- a Main achievements
- b Introduction, with a short summary about the person
- c Conclusion, with a personal opinion
- d Other things the person has done

▶ **Subskill: Using conjunctions – *because, so, although***

We use conjunctions to join two parts of sentences, e.g. *They couldn't wash their hands **although** they wanted to.*

3 Look at the conjunctions in bold in the text. Answer the questions.
1 Which do we use …
   - a to contrast information?
   - b to talk about results or purposes?
   - c to give a reason?
2 Which can come either at the beginning of a sentence or in the middle?

4 Read the notes about Rebecca Constantino. Complete the sentences with *because, so* or *although*.

- While she was researching literacy, Rebecca discovered school libraries in poor areas were terrible. Young people didn't have access to interesting books **1** (…) they were doing worse at school.
- Rebecca set up the non-profit Access Books **2** (…) she wanted to improve school libraries in poor areas.
- Many of the libraries were in poor condition **3** (…) the group decorated them.
- The group also offers author visits **4** (…) they want to interest young people in books and writing.
- **5** (…) the schools had some books, they were old and in bad condition.
- The group wants local people to get involved **6** (…) they ask students, parents and staff to help decorate the libraries.

QUICK REVIEW 1

5 Join the sentences with *because*, *so* or *although*. Make any necessary changes and take care with punctuation.

1. Rebecca's organisation has provided over 1.5 million books. She wants to do more.
2. Her work certainly made me think. I didn't realise there was a problem.
3. In my opinion, Rebecca's work is making a difference. She has helped to improve literacy.
4. You might not know Rebecca's name. She is someone I admire and she inspires me.
5. Now, young people in these schools are more interested in reading. They do better at school.

6 Read the sentences in exercises 4 and 5 again and write a profile of Rebecca Constantino. Follow the steps in the Skills boost.

SKILLS BOOST

THINK
Write notes about Rebecca Constantino's life and achievements.

PREPARE
Organise your notes into paragraphs.
Paragraph 1 Introduction, with a short summary about the person
Paragraph 2 Main achievements
Paragraph 3 Other things the person has done
Paragraph 4 Conclusion, with a personal opinion

WRITE
Write your profile. Use the model profile and your notes to help you.

CHECK
Read your profile. Answer the questions.
1. Have you organised your information into clear paragraphs?
2. Have you used *because*, *so* and *although* correctly to join ideas?
3. Have you used the past simple and past continuous correctly?
4. Have you included vocabulary about helping people and personality adjectives?

7 Exchange your profile with another student. Answer the questions.
1. Did the writer include interesting information about the person?
2. Is the profile well organised?
3. Did the profile make you want to find out more about Rebecca Constantino?

Grammar

Past simple, past continuous and *used to*
We use the past simple to talk about finished actions in the past.
I/you/he/she/we/they **developed** projects.
I/you/he/she/we/they **didn't develop** projects.
Did I/you/he/she/we/they **develop** projects?
We use the past continuous to talk about actions in progress at a time in the past.
I/he/she **was volunteering**/**wasn't volunteering**.
You/we/they **were volunteering**/**weren't volunteering**.
Was I/he/she **volunteering**?
Were you/we/they **volunteering**?
We use *used to* to talk about past habits and states.
The school libraries **used to** be in poor condition. Young people **didn't use to** have access to many books.

when, while
After *when* we usually use the past simple. After *while*, we usually use the past continuous.
When she arrived, she took off her coat.
The ball hit his head **while** he was playing baseball.
He was playing baseball **when** the ball hit his head.

Subject and object questions
Subject questions
In subject questions, the question word is the subject of the question. We do not use an auxiliary verb.
Who started the company?
What happened?

Object questions
In object questions, the question word is the object of the question. We use an auxiliary verb.
Who **did** she **help**?
What **does** she **do**?

Vocabulary

🔊 7 **Personality adjectives**
brave, calm, careful, confident, creative, curious, enthusiastic, friendly, funny, generous, hard-working, kind, patient, pleasant, positive, quiet, reliable, sensible, sociable, talented

🔊 8 **Verb and noun collocations: helping others**
achieve a goal, change society, encourage a friend, gain knowledge, help others, make a difference, sign an online petition, start a campaign, support other people, win an award

21

Project

WDYT? (What do you think?) **Who inspires you?**

TASK: Create a video about an inspiring person.

Learning outcomes
1. I can make a video presentation about someone who inspires me.
2. I can communicate clearly, using oral, written and non-verbal communication.
3. I can use appropriate language from the unit.

Graphic organiser → Project planner p118

1 🎥 Watch a video of students talking about people who inspire them. Who do they mention?

STEP 1: THINK ◼︎◻︎◻︎◻︎

2 What makes someone inspiring? Think about the people in this unit.

3 Read the video presentation notes in the Model project. Which one piece of information do they <u>not</u> include?
- the names of the people
- who the people are and what they are like
- their achievements
- why the speaker thinks they are inspiring
- where the people were born and their complete life history
- the speaker's opinion about things/people

STEP 2: PLAN ◼︎◼︎◻︎◻︎

4 Choose your inspiring person. It can be a famous person or someone you know. Research him/her and make notes. Use the list in exercise 3 to help you.

5 Decide how to organise your information. Try to include appropriate grammar and vocabulary.

STEP 3: CREATE ◼︎◼︎◼︎◻︎

6 Work in pairs. Read the tips in the Super skills box and practise saying the Key phrases with a partner.

COMMUNICATION

Verbal and non-verbal communication

Tips
1. **Verbal:** Speak directly to the audience. Speak clearly and vary your tone and speed.
2. **Non-verbal:** Have good eye contact, smile and don't cross your arms. Use gestures and facial expressions to help show meaning.

Key phrases
Remember to (sit up).
You should/shouldn't (look at the ground).
You didn't (smile).
You need to (speak more clearly).
How about (speaking more slowly)? / Why don't you (speak louder)?

7 Read the *How to …* tips on p118. Practise first, then record your video. Use the tips and Key phrases in the Super skills box.

Grammar and Vocabulary → Quick review p21

Model project

Who inspires me? Zayn Malik! He's a talented singer and songwriter. He used to be in the band One Direction but now he creates his own music. People think that he has the perfect life, but he also suffers from anxiety. He tells his fans when it's a problem and I think it's really important that celebrities talk about this to help raise awareness about well-being.

I think Jason Barnes is really inspiring. He wanted to be a world class drummer but he lost an arm in an accident. A scientist designed a special robot arm for him that holds two drumsticks. It allows him to drum better than most other drummers. Jason is now studying music and hopes to be a professional musician. He's creative and hard-working and he makes me feel that I could achieve anything!

Melati and Isabel Wijsen are two amazing sisters from Bali in Indonesia. They started their own company in 2013 called Bye Bye Plastic Bags when they were only 10 and 12. They asked people to help clean up beaches and sign petitions to stop using plastic bags. They worked very hard and there are now no plastic bags in Bali. They want to do the same thing in other countries. We think that's really inspiring!

STEP 4: PRESENT

8 Show your video to the class. Answer your classmates' questions about it.

9 `Peer review` Watch your classmates' videos.
   1. Who did you think was the most inspiring person? Why?
   2. What did you like about your classmates' videos? Why?

1 FINAL REFLECTION

1. **The task**
   How well have you done the task?

2. **Super skills**
   Did you pay attention to your verbal and non-verbal communication?

3. **Language**
   What language did you use from the unit? Give examples.

Beyond the task
Does hearing or reading about an inspiring person make you want to do things differently? Why/Why not?

2 Love to learn!

(What do you think?)

What's the best new skill you've ever learnt, and how can you teach it to others?

Vocabulary: skills and abilities (including past participle forms); learning techniques

Grammar: present perfect with *for/since/How long/just/yet/already*; present perfect and past simple

Reading: online reviews about learning new skills

Listening: a podcast about learning languages

Speaking: asking for and giving information

Writing: a blog

Project: a tutorial for learning a new skill

Video skills p25

Real-world speaking p31

Project pp34–35

1 I have never ridden a quad-bike or a go-kart.

2 I have never learnt to sew or knit.

3 I have never written computer code.

4 I have never climbed an indoor climbing wall

Skills and abilities

1 ♻ Match the 'I have never' cards 1–6 with pictures A–F. Which ones are true for you?

2 Which four cards contain irregular past participles? How are the regular past participles formed?

3 Find the infinitive form of the irregular past participles in the box. You can look at p126.

| built   caught   done   driven   learnt   ridden |
| spoken   sung   swum   written |

Vocabulary 2

6 Complete the diagram with the words in the box. Then add expressions from exercise 4.

> an app   a moped   a mountain   ~~a poem~~

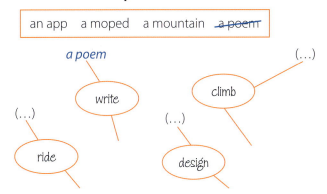

7 Invent four new 'I have never' cards with sentences that are true for you. Use verbs from exercise 3 or your own ideas.

> **I have never** swum in the Atlantic Ocean.

8 Work in groups of four. Put all your cards face down in the middle and take turns to read a card. The first person to say 'I have!' wins the card if he/she can give more information about it.

> I have! I swam in the Atlantic when I was on holiday in Portugal.

5 **I have never** done DIY.

6 **I have never** played in an orchestra.

9 🎥 Watch the video. What three things does Sophie want to do?

10 💬 Work in pairs. Discuss the questions.
1 Why do vloggers make this type of video?
2 What makes the video interesting and attractive? Think about music, images, colour, light, and the vlogger.

4 🎯 🔊 9 Listen and repeat the skills and abilities. How many of the things in the box can you do?

> bake bread   build a robot   catch a fish
> climb an indoor climbing wall
> design (your own) clothes
> do DIY (do-it-yourself)   drive a vehicle
> learn a foreign language   learn to sew
> ride a quad-bike   sing in a choir
> swim 20 lengths   write computer code

5 🔊 10 Listen to Jessica answer ten questions. How many of the activities has she done?

25

2 Reading and critical thinking

Online reviews

1 Choose one or two new skills that you want to learn during the next school holidays. Where can you learn these skills?

2 Skim the reviews on p27. Which of the skills in the box are they about?

> climbing   cooking   driving   first aid   robotics

▶ **Subskill: Scanning for specific information**

When you scan a text, you read it very quickly to look for specific information. It doesn't matter if you don't understand all the words.

3 Read the subskill information. Then scan the reviews and copy and complete the table.

Activity week	1	2	3
Age	1 (…)	2 (…)	3 (…)
Number of days	4 (…)	5 (…)	6 (…)

4 🔊 11 Read and listen to the text. Make a list of at least three new skills that Alice, Ben and Cora have learnt during the activity weeks.

Alice: how to *drive*, (…)
Ben: how to (…)
Cora: how to (…)

5 **Word work** Find words or expressions in the text that mean:
1 try new ideas or methods (v)
2 practical (adj)
3 drive (an expression with v+n)
4 become an expert at something (v)
5 when you live at the place you're studying (adj)
6 not on real roads (adj)

6 Read the text again and answer the questions.
1 Why hasn't Alice passed her test yet?
2 What other activities did Alice try?
3 Did Ben stay in a hotel?
4 What did Ben do after the cookery course?
5 How did Cora test her robot?
6 What other Fire Tech courses are there?

7 Write questions for the answers about Alice, Ben and Cora. Start with the words in brackets.
1 (What kind …)
She drove a Mini Cooper.
2 (How old …)
She's 14.
3 (Can Ben …)
Yes, he can. He learnt on the course.
4 (Could Ben …)
No, he couldn't. There wasn't any Wi-Fi.
5 (What …)
She learnt to design and build robots.
6 (Did Cora …)
Yes, she did. She had a great week!

8 💬 Work in pairs. Have you ever done any of the activities mentioned in the online review?

> Have you ever learnt to cook?
>
> Yes, I have! My parents taught me.
>
> Have you ever baked bread?
>
> No, I haven't but I must learn.

CRITICAL THINKING

1 Understand Think about the courses on p27. Which one sounds most interesting to you? Write sentences.
I'd like to …
I'm not sure about …
I don't fancy …

2 Analyse Examine your preferred options. What are the advantages and disadvantages?

3 Evaluate Decide which course sounds most interesting to you. Explain your reasons and how you reached your decision.
I'd like to do the (…) course because (…).

Research

Find out more about other activity courses in your town/country. Are there any that inspire you more than the one you chose in Critical Thinking?

Learn new skills!
Reviews: Amazing activity weeks

There are some great activity weeks out there, but don't just take our word for it – find out what the participants have said!

🔍 Search: **UK**

❶ PGL Learner Driver Course
Boreatton Park, Shropshire ★★★★★

Have you always wanted to learn to drive, but you haven't turned 17 yet? Don't worry – this six-day activity course is for 13–16-year-olds! As I've wanted to **get behind the wheel** for years, this was the perfect opportunity! I really was allowed to drive a proper car – a Mini Cooper, no less! Obviously we didn't drive on real roads, but we had plenty of practice every morning at a special **off-road** location. Have I passed my test yet? No, I haven't – unfortunately that's not legal yet! But I have learnt how to drive and park the car, and how to pass the theory test. As well as that, I tried quad-biking and go-karting, and made some great new friends! 😄

Alice (14)

❷ Root Camp Cookery Course
Locations include Hereford, Suffolk, Scotland ★★★★★

Whether you've been a mini-chef for years or you've just started cooking, I'd definitely recommend Root Camp. I've learnt to bake bread, catch fish and survive for a week without Wi-Fi! 😂 Honestly, it was great fun meeting everyone else and camping on the Isle of Bute in Scotland. I've enjoyed cooking since I was a kid, but I never realised it could be so creative! This course has definitely inspired me. Since coming home, I've **experimented** with some new dishes. I've uploaded photos of them on Instagram – have a look here! (By the way, this six-day **residential** course is for 15–21-year-olds.)

Ben (16)

❸ Fire Tech Robotics Course
Lancing College, Brighton ★★★★★

I've just finished a Robotics course at Fire Tech. What an amazing week! If you've ever wanted **to master** robotics, this is the course for you. I've learnt to design my own robot, build it using a VEX IQ kit, and program it in the ROBOTC language. It was very **hands-on** and we tested our robots in real competitions. We worked in teams and it was really exciting to see whose robots would win. I also learnt to write computer code. This one-week course is for under-17s, and other Fire Tech courses include app design, video game design and digital music production. I've already put them on my wish list!

Cora (15)

Write your review here.

The longer read → Resource centre

2 Grammar

Present perfect with *for*, *since* and *How long ...?*

1 Read the examples and complete the rules. How do you say *for* and *since* in your language?

> How long has Alice wanted to drive?
> She's wanted to drive for years.
> How long has Ben enjoyed cooking?
> He's enjoyed cooking since he was a kid.

1 We use the present perfect with (…) to talk about the point in time when an action starts.
2 We use the present perfect with (…) to talk about the duration of an action.

2 Copy and complete the table with the phrases in the box. Then add two more of your own.

> 2017   eight o'clock   this morning   a long time
> a week   ages   an hour   I was 12   last week
> Monday   two years

For	Since
an hour	last week

3 🔊 12 Choose the correct words. Then listen and check your answers.

Max Polhill **1 loves/has loved** technology **2 for/since** many years – **3 for/since** he got his first computer at the age of two! Soon he began to write computer code, and in 2012 he designed his first game app, *Stellar Alien*. Since then, he **4 creates/has created** many games, music videos and animations. Max **5 runs/has run** his own company, Xavier Games, **6 for/since** the age of 14.

4 Complete the sentences with information that is true for you. Use the present perfect and *for* or *since*.

1 *I've been in this room for 30 minutes.*
2 I … (have) this book for/since …
3 Our teacher … (teach) us English …
4 I … (study) English …
5 We … (be) at this school …
6 I … (live) in my house …

5 💬 Work in pairs. Make questions with *How long …* for the sentences in exercise 4. Ask and answer.

> How long have you been in this room?
> I've been in this room for 20 minutes – I was late for class!

just, *yet* and *already*

6 Read the examples and choose the correct option in rules 1–6.

> Alice has just learnt to drive.
> Has she passed her test yet?
> Cora has already built a robot.
> She hasn't designed an app yet.

1 We put *yet* at the **start/end** of the sentence.
2 We put *already* and *just* **before/after** the past participle.
3 We use *yet* in **affirmative/negative** sentences and questions.
4 We use **just/yet** to talk about something that happened very recently.
5 We use **yet/already** for something that happened previously or sooner than expected.
6 We use **just/yet** to say or ask whether something that we expected has happened or not.

7 Rewrite the sentences adding the word in brackets. Are they true or false for you?

1 We've done exercise 6. (already)
2 We haven't solved the puzzle. (yet)
3 We've learnt the present perfect. (already)
4 The bell hasn't rung. (yet)

8 Answer the question to solve the Brain teaser.

Jill, Phil and Will are triplets who all love running, and have just turned 16. Jill and Phil have just joined an Athletic Club, although they've enjoyed running since they were 12. Will hasn't joined the club yet, but he's already been a runner for six years. They often run 5 k races together, but Jill and Phil have just run a 10 k race, too. None of them has run a marathon yet, but Jill has already won a half-marathon!

1 Who started running first?
2 Who has run the furthest?

Vocabulary and Listening 2

Learning techniques

1 Look at the learning techniques. Which of them have you used in your English class, and which in self-study?

In class, I've taken notes and (…)
In self-study, I've used apps and (…)

> do a conversation exchange   draw mind maps
> follow instructions   highlight key points
> keep practising   listen to podcasts
> learn (something) by heart   record yourself
> revise for a test   set up a study group
> take a course (in something)   take notes
> use sticky notes   use apps   watch video tutorials

Confusable words
revise (UK) = review (US)
study something again before a test

2 Categorise the words in exercise 1 according to which skills are used. Some words could go in more than one category.

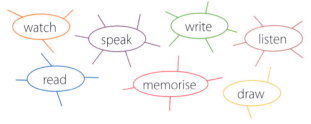

3 🔊 13 Change pictures 1–8 for words or expressions from exercise 1. Then listen, check and repeat.

A podcast

4 🔊 14 Look at the information about the podcast. Which things do you think you will hear? Listen and check.
  a people speaking in lots of different languages
  b people speaking about how they've learnt foreign languages

Let's speak a foreign language!
To celebrate our 50th podcast, tell us what you've loved so far, and send us your top tips!

▶ **Subskill: Remembering what you hear**
Sometimes it's a good idea to take notes while you're listening. Focus on the key information that you need to answer the questions.

5 Read the subskill information. Then listen again. Take notes so you can answer the questions about each of speakers 1–5.
  1 Which language is he/she learning?
  2 Which learning method is he/she using?

6 Listen again and complete the sentences.
  1 Jacob practises every morning while (…) .
  2 Anya and her friends have memorised (…) .
  3 Cathy loves watching (…) .
  4 Rashid started learning a new language in (…) .
  5 Nuala met Almudena when (…) .

7 Have you ever used any of the techniques for learning English? What tip(s) would you add to the podcast?

How to be a top student

The key to being a top student is to be consistent through the year. Think about the things that help you learn – for example, **1** (…) in class and **2** (…) the key points, or **3** (…) the class and listen again later. You can also watch video tutorials about your subject.

If you're learning a new language, you could use **4** (…) to practise your pronunciation, or do a **5** (…) in person or by video call. A good tip for learning vocabulary is to draw **6** (…) to group the words. You can also put **7** (…) around the house!

If you prefer to study with others, you could set up a **8** (…) when you have to revise for an exam. And remember: don't just learn everything by heart – you need to understand it too!

2 Grammar

Present perfect and past simple

1 Match rules 1–3 with examples a–f.

> a Have you ever done a conversation exchange?
> b Nuala went to Spain last summer.
> c Her school organised an exchange a year ago.
> d Rashid started learning Mandarin in September.
> e Anya has already learnt ten songs by heart.
> f We've studied English for years.

1 We use the past simple for an action completed at a specific time in the past.
2 We use the present perfect for an action that started in the past and continues or is still relevant now.
3 We use the present perfect for an action that happened at an unspecified time in the past.

2 Copy and complete the table with the time expressions from exercise 1. Then add the expressions in the box.

> at the age of   in (+ month / year)   just
> never   since   yesterday   yet

Time expressions	
with past simple	with present perfect
last	ever

3 🔊 15 Complete the text with time expressions from exercise 2. Then listen and check. How many different ways can Bibi say hello?

Have you **1** ever heard of Bibi the African parrot? A friend of mine has **2** (…) shown me a video of her online. Apparently Bibi has loved languages **3** (…) she was born. **4** (…) two she already knew a lot of words, and now she can say 'hello' in 20 different languages, including Polish, Japanese and Swahili. Bibi was born **5** (…) 2006, but she's still young for a parrot; they can live up to 60 years. Bibi also does great sound effects. She can sound like a dog, cat or chicken. I've **6** (…) seen anything like it!

4 Complete the sentences with the past simple or present perfect form of the verbs.

1 We (…) **(use)** this book since September.
2 I (…) **(speak)** a foreign language yesterday.
3 I (…) **(come)** to this school when I was 12.
4 We (…) **(have)** five English classes last week.
5 I (…) **(never / watch)** a YouTube tutorial.

5 Complete the questions with the correct form of the past simple or the present perfect.

1 a (…) **(you / speak)** English all your life?
   b When (…) **(you / start)** to learn English?
2 a (…) **(you / always have)** the same English teacher?
   b Who (…) **(be)** your English teacher last year?
3 a (…) **(you / always be)** a student at this school?
   b Which primary school (…) **(you / go)** to?

6 💬 Work in pairs. Ask and answer the questions in exercise 5.

7 Choose the correct option.

> **GRAMMAR ROUND-UP**
> 1 2 3 4 5 6 7 8
>
> ### 'Stayin' alive': can karaoke save endangered languages?
>
> Have you **1 ever try/tried ever/ever tried** singing karaoke? In Spokane, Washington (USA), karaoke is more than a fun night out — it's a way of keeping the indigenous Salish language alive. Every year they **2 have/had/are having** a karaoke competition to encourage people to use the endangered Native American language.
>
> In the past, thousands of people **3 were speaking/speak/spoke** Salish, but now only about 300 people **4 speak/are speaking/have spoken** it fluently. Karaoke judge Grahm Wiley-Camacho learnt a dialect of Salish while he **5 grew/was growing/has grown** up. He **6 speaks/spoke/has spoken** the language since he was a child, and now he's trying to keep it alive by teaching others. After studying Salish **7 since/for/ago** only nine months, Keegan Heron **8 wins/won/was winning** second prize in the competition with his version of 'Everybody' by the Backstreet Boys, translated into Salish.

> **Research**
>
> Find out more about karaoke. When and where did it begin?

Real-world speaking 2

Asking for information

1 Look at the picture. Where do you think they are? What kind of activity is Joe interested in?

2 🎥 Watch the video and answer the questions. What activity does Joe want to do?

Joe
Hello, I'm looking for information about one of the after-school activities.

Receptionist
Yes, of course. Which activity are you interested in?

Joe
The rock choir. I think it's on **1 Tuesday/Thursday** evenings?

Receptionist
Ah, yes. Have you sung in a choir before?

Joe
No, I haven't. I started singing a couple of **2 months/years** ago, though.

Receptionist
No problem. This choir is for everyone!

Joe
Great! Has the new term already started?

Receptionist
No, they haven't started yet so it's the perfect time to register.

Joe
I've heard it's very popular. Do I need to sign up now?

Receptionist
Yes, that would be best. It filled up quite quickly last year.

Joe
Ah, I've got one more question. What time is it on?

Receptionist
It's from 4:15 to **3 5:15/5:45**.

Joe
Great. Thanks for your help.

Receptionist
You're welcome! Just ask if you need any more information.

3 Watch again and choose the correct options.

4 Read the Key phrases. Which phrases are about asking for information, and which are about giving information?

5 Create your own dialogue. Follow the steps in the Skills boost.

SKILLS BOOST

THINK
Look at the pictures and choose the class you'd like to find out about. Make notes about the day/time/level/price.

PREPARE
Prepare a dialogue. Remember to include phrases for asking for and giving information.

PRACTISE
Practise your dialogue. Remember to use appropriate intonation for sounding polite.

PERFORM
Act out your dialogue for the class.

6 **Peer review** Listen to your classmates. Answer the questions.
  1 Which classes did they want to do?
  2 How many of the useful phrases did they use?
  3 Did they sound polite?

Key phrases
I'm looking for information about …
Have you … before?
I've heard it's very popular.
Do I need to sign up now?
I've got one more question.
Thanks for your help.
Just ask if you need any more information.

Phrasebook → p122

2 Writing

Give it a go!
Learn how to make your own accessories

FAQs | **BLOG** | Tutorials | Forum | Competitions | Subscribe | Login / register

What's your skill?

In today's post, Vala tells us about her latest craft project: personalised accessories.

1 How long have you been interested in this activity?
I've designed my own T-shirts since I was about 13. Then last year I started doing accessories, too – mainly bags and trainers.

2 How did you learn?
I did a design course a couple of years ago. Then I practised a lot! Also, I sometimes read other people's blogs, and I often watch video tutorials on YouTube.

3 What has been your proudest moment yet?
I sold one of my designs! One of my friends bought a bag that I personalised. Lots of my friends have asked me to make things for them.

4 What are you working on now?
At the moment, I'm making a rucksack for my brother's birthday. I've just sewn the patches on – I hope he likes it!

5 How did you get inspired?
While I was staying with my grandparents one summer, they taught me to sew and to do DIY. Ever since then, I've loved making things.

> **Who, How, Where?**
> - **Is this skill for everyone?** Absolutely! All you need is lots of creativity and an eye for detail.
> - **How do you learn?** It's easy to teach yourself with video tutorials. You could also find out if there are any craft and design classes where you live.
> - **Get inspired!** Find craft tutorials and blogs about sewing online.

A blog

1 Read the blog. What are Vala's skills? How did she learn them?

2 Read the blog again and complete the sentences.
   1. Vala has designed her own T-shirts since (…) .
   2. Vala often (…) .
   3. Vala sold a bag to (…) .
   4. (…) have asked her to make things for them.
   5. Vala is making a rucksack for (…) .
   6. (…) taught her to sew and do DIY.

▶ **Subskill: Using tenses correctly**

Sometimes the time expression can help you decide which tense to use.

3 Read the subskill information. Match the verbs in bold in sentences 1–5 with the tenses a–e. How do you say the time expressions in your language?

1. I **did** a design course a couple of years ago.
2. I sometimes **read** other people's blogs.
3. At the moment, I**'m making** a rucksack.
4. I**'ve** just **sewn** on the patches.
5. While I **was staying** with my grandparents, they **taught** me to sew and do DIY.

a present simple
b present continuous
c past simple
d past continuous; past simple
e present perfect

4 Find three more examples in the blog of the present simple, past simple and present perfect. Which time expressions can you find?

5 Complete sentences a–e with the correct tense of the verbs in brackets. Then match them with questions 1–5 in the blog.

a   I first got inspired while I (…) **(watch)** indoor climbing on TV.
b   At the moment I (…) **(prepare)** to take the National Indoor Climbing award.
c   I (…) **(do)** a climbing course with Scouts last summer.
d   I (…) **(be)** interested in climbing for about a year.
e   I (…) **(just / complete)** my most difficult climb – my friend helped me get there.

6 Write a blog about a skill that you've learnt. Follow the steps in the Skills boost.

SKILLS BOOST

THINK
Choose the skill that you're going to write about. Think about your answers to questions 1-5 in the blog.

PREPARE
Make notes to answer the five questions about your skill.
Give additional information for the 'Who, How, Where?' section of the blog.

WRITE
Write your blog. Use the model and your notes to help you.

CHECK
Read your blog. Answer the questions.
1 Have you used the correct tenses?
2 Have you included time expressions that go with the present simple, present continuous, past simple and present perfect?
3 Have you checked the spelling of irregular verb forms?
4 Have you included vocabulary about skills and abilities and learning techniques?

7 **Peer review** Exchange your blog with another student. Answer the questions.
1 Did he/she answer all five questions in the blog?
2 Did he/she use the correct tenses?
3 Did he/she give information about how you could learn this skill?

QUICK REVIEW

Grammar

Present perfect
➕ *I've learnt to write computer code.*
➖ *I haven't learnt to cook.*
❓ *Have you learnt to make bread?*
Yes, I have. / No, I haven't.

for*, *since* and *How long …?
We use *since* to talk about the point in time when an action starts.
How long has Ben enjoyed cooking?
*He's enjoyed cooking **since** he was young.*
We use *for* to talk about the duration of an action.
How long has Alice wanted to drive?
*She's wanted to drive **for** years.*

just*, *yet* and *already
We use *just* to talk about something that happened very recently.
*Alice has **just** learnt to drive.*
We use *yet* to ask whether something that we expected has happened or to say that something hasn't happened.
*Has she bought a car **yet**?*
*She hasn't passed her test **yet**.*
We use *already* for something that happened previously or sooner than expected.
*Ben has **already** experimented with some new dishes.*

Present perfect and past simple
We use the past simple for an action completed at a specific time in the past.
*Nuala went to Spain **last** summer.*
*Her school organised an exchange a year **ago**.*
*Rashid started learning Mandarin **in** September.*
We use the present perfect for an action that happened at an unspecified time in the past, or an action that started in the past and continues or is still relevant now.
*Have you **ever** done a conversation exchange?*
*Anya has **already** learnt ten songs by heart.*
*We've studied English **for** years.*

Vocabulary

🔊 16 **Skills and abilities**
bake bread, build a robot, catch a fish, climb an indoor climbing wall, do DIY (do-it-yourself), design (your own) clothes, drive a vehicle, learn a foreign language, learn to knit, learn to sew, play in an orchestra, ride a go-kart, ride a quad-bike, sing in a choir, swim 20 lengths, write computer code

🔊 17 **Learning techniques**
do a conversation exchange, draw mind maps, follow instructions, highlight key points, keep practising, learn (something) by heart, listen to podcasts, record yourself, revise for a test, set up a study group, take a course (in something), take notes, use apps, use sticky notes, watch video tutorials

33

2 Project

(What do you think?)

What's the best new skill you've ever learnt, and how can you teach it to others?

TASK: Create a tutorial to teach your classmates a new skill.

Learning outcomes
1 I can prepare and teach a tutorial about a new skill.
2 I can think critically to find the best solution for a problem.
3 I can use appropriate language from the unit.

Graphic organiser → Project planner p118

1 🎥 Watch a video tutorial. Practise saying the words.

STEP 1: THINK ●○○○

2 Read the Model project and follow the instructions.
  1 Brainstorm all the skills you know.
  2 Which of the different methods in the box could you use to teach these skills? Can you think of other ways?

  > app   face-to-face teaching
  > podcast   video tutorial

3 Look at the Model project again. What method do they use to teach their skill?

STEP 2: PLAN ●●○○

4 Work in pairs. Read the tips in the Super skills box and practise saying the Key phrases with a partner.

CRITICAL THINKING

Finding the best solution for a problem

Tips
Identify the problem and understand everyone's needs and challenges.
Brainstorm possible solutions and choose the best one.
Carry out your plan and evaluate its success.

Key phrases
What's the best way to …?
How useful is …?
How shall we …?
We/they won't be able to …
Do you think we should …?
Let's …!
What about trying …?

5 Work in pairs. Follow the instructions.
  1 Choose:
     a one of your skills from exercise 2
     or
     b how to say 'Hello' in five more languages.
  2 Decide on the best method for your tutorial. Use the tips and Key phrases in the Super skills box.

STEP 3: CREATE ●●●○

6 Read the *How to …* tips on p118. Then create your tutorial.

7 Practise teaching your tutorial with your partner. Record yourselves, and make any necessary changes.

34   Grammar and Vocabulary → Quick review p33

Model project

We've all studied English for years. But it can be hard to learn a new language! Have you ever wanted to talk to people in other languages?

In this video tutorial, we're going to teach you how to say 'Hello!' in five other foreign languages.

Are you ready? We're going to take you through the steps now.

You'll see the word and hear us say it. And then you repeat the word! Ready?

Bonjour!

你好
Nǐ hao

Guten Tag!

こんにちは
Kon'nichiwa!

Здравствуйте!
Zdravstvutye!

How to teach anyone anything!

Whether you're teaching someone to sing, sew, bake bread or speak a foreign language, follow these steps and your classmates will soon master a new skill!

1 Tell	Have you explained the learning objective?	
2 Show	Have you demonstrated the new skill?	
3 Practise	Have your classmates had the chance to practise the skill?	
4 Review	Have you reviewed their progress?	

STEP 4: PRESENT ■■■■

8 With your partner, give your tutorial to another pair, or show them your tutorial video.

9 **Peer review** Take turns. Follow the other pair's tutorial. What new skill did you learn?

2 FINAL REFLECTION

1 **The task**
How successfully did other students learn from your tutorial?

2 **Super skills**
How did you find the best solutions for any possible problems while you were planning your tutorial?

3 **Language**
Did you use new language from this unit? Give examples.

Beyond the task
Do you think all skills can be learnt? Why/Why not?

35

3 Look after yourself

WDYT?
(What do you think?)

How can you improve your health?

Vocabulary: staying healthy: health and well-being; healthy habits

Grammar: modal verbs; gerund and infinitive

Reading: an advice page about healthy eating

Listening: an informal conversation about heatlhy habits

Speaking: giving instructions

Writing: an informal email

Project: a fitness diary

Video skills p37

Real-world speaking p43

Project pp46–47

Staying healthy

1 Look at the list of ways to stay healthy. Can you add any more?

do exercise	eat fruit and vegetables
have a healthy diet	watch less TV
play sports	eat less sugar

2 Work in pairs. Talk about the ways to stay healthy in exercise 1. Use *always, often, usually, sometimes, hardly ever, never*.

I often play sports.

My brother never eats fruit!

36

There's an app for it!

Vocabulary 3

 It's important to **drink enough water**. Try *Waterlogged* – the app lets you record how much you're drinking. You set your own goals!

 The *Fooducate* app scans barcodes to see how nutritional the items really are. So you won't want to **eat fast food**!

 Running is a good way to **spend time outdoors** and helps you to **keep fit**. *Spring* is a great app with over 35,000 songs. You can use it to do any exercise – so **get active**!

 Do you often **go to bed late** and wake up tired? Make sure you **get enough sleep** by using an app like *Sleep Cycle*.

 If you ever **feel stressed**, then *Headspace* is the app for you! It offers relaxation techniques and meditation activities that can **improve your mood**, so you feel happier and calmer.

 Do you ever **skip breakfast**? *Meal Reminders* helps you to eat regularly and not miss out meals. That way, you don't feel tempted to **have sugary snacks**. Remember not to **eat too quickly** either.

Health and well-being

3 Read about the health apps. Choose the best app for each problem 1–6. Which sentences describe you?

1. I'm sometimes tired in the morning.
2. I love music and want to be physically stronger.
3. I feel worried and tense before exams.
4. I often forget to drink enough water.
5. I'd like to know more about good nutrition.
6. I sometimes forget to eat in the morning.

4 Read the texts again. Look at the expressions in bold and find words that mean:
1. containing a lot of sugar
2. affected by a worried or nervous feeling
3. the way that someone is feeling, e.g. happy or sad
4. avoid doing something
5. a small amount of food you eat between meals
6. food that is made and served quickly, e.g. burgers
7. make something better
8. healthy, strong and able to do physical exercise

5 Answer the questions.
1. Why is it important to spend time outdoors?
2. What do you do when you feel stressed?
3. How much sleep do you get?
4. What do you do to improve your mood?
5. How do you keep fit?

6 Complete the sentences with words and phrases related to health and well-being.

Three things I often do are (…).
Two things I would like to do more often are (…).
One thing I'd like to do less often is (…).

7 Compare your answers with a partner. Find out more information.

> I often play sports, drink plenty of water and go to bed late.

> Which sports do you play?

VIDEO SKILLS

8 Watch the video. What different sports and activities do you see?

9 Work in pairs. Discuss the questions.
1. Why are 'top 5' videos popular?
2. Do you like this type of video? Why/Why not?

Pronunciation: short /ɒ/ and long /ɔː/ → p116

3 Reading and critical thinking

An advice page

1 Look at the title of the text and the photos. Which expressions from pp36–37 do you think will be in the text? Scan the text and check your ideas.

2 Read the text quickly and choose the best summary.

The text is giving advice about
a food to help you feel and think better.
b food that helps you perform better at sports.
c the best kinds of food for young people to eat.

▶ **Subskill: Understanding new words**

First, look at the sentence the word is in. Can you guess the meaning from the sentence? Next, look at the sentences before and after. Can they help you guess the meaning?

3 **Word work** Follow the steps in the subskill to guess the best meaning for the words in bold in the text.

1 affect
   a pretend   b change or influence
2 rise
   a increase   b decrease
3 boost
   a help increase   b negatively affect
4 steady
   a staying the same   b changing level
5 release
   a stop   b make available
6 cheer up
   a make happy   b annoy
7 regulate
   a work slower   b control something

4 🔊 18 Read and listen to the text. Are the statements true, false or is there no information in the text? Correct the false statements.

1 Food only affects your body, not your brain.
2 Dark chocolate contains a lot of magnesium.
3 The magnesium in mangoes keeps you calm.
4 In one study, students who drank blueberry juice every day for a week performed better.
5 Fish and seafood contain vitamin B.
6 Fish and legumes don't contain much protein.

5 Choose the correct answers.

1 When you eat dark chocolate,
   a it's important to take care with the amount.
   b you will immediately feel happier and calmer.
   c it causes problems with your blood sugar.
2 If you want to remember things,
   a you need to eat blueberries regularly.
   b use rosemary oil when you are studying.
   c drink juice rather than eating blueberries.
3 When you don't drink enough water,
   a your mood will be much worse.
   b it will not affect your memory.
   c you will find it more difficult to focus.
4 If you don't get enough B vitamins, you
   a are often likely to feel hungry between meals.
   b will have low energy, but will be happy.
   c should eat more foods like beans and fish.
5 According to the text, nuts
   a are a good slow-energy-release food.
   b can make you feel more cheerful.
   c are better than proteins or wholegrains.
6 You should eat eggs and bananas
   a because they contain a lot of serotonin.
   b only four times a week.
   c to help your body produce serotonin.

6 💬 Work in pairs. Answer the question.

Have you tried any foods that have helped you feel better?

CRITICAL THINKING   *SUPER SKILLS*

1 **Understand** Choose three foods, drinks or oils mentioned in the text and explain what each one is good for. Which one do you think is the most useful for you?
2 **Apply** What information would you include in a sketch or advert to tell people about a food, drink or oil's health benefits? Describe how you would make people want to use it.
3 **Create** Prepare a short sketch or advert about the food to illustrate how it can help with a problem.

Research

Find more information about other foods or drinks that are good for each of the categories in the text. Which are most interesting for you?

Mind what you eat!

Everyone knows that a healthy diet is good for your body, but it's also good for your mind. Research has shown that the brain and digestive system are closely connected. Eating the right foods can **affect** the way you feel and think. Luckily, you don't have to make many changes to have an impact. Here are a few suggestions – look online for other ideas!

You're feeling stressed or anxious

Foods that are high in magnesium (Mg) make you feel calmer. Dark chocolate is good, but you mustn't eat more than 50g or your blood sugar will **rise** quickly and then fall. This causes low mood! A handful of almonds (around 12) will give you about 20% of your recommended daily intake (RDI) of magnesium. Mangoes are a great fruit for increasing calm. They contain a chemical called linalool that reduces stress. Reducing or cutting out fast food and sugary snacks also helps.

You've got a test or you need to concentrate

Blueberries can help to **boost** your brain function. In one study, students performed tasks 10% faster and more accurately after drinking blueberry juice. In another, researchers found that people were able to do 15% better in memory tests if they could smell rosemary oil when they studied. Remember to drink enough water – around a litre a day. Dehydration can cause low energy and mood changes so it's hard to motivate yourself to study, focus or remember information.

You've got no energy

The body can't get or make energy without B vitamins. Foods with vitamin B include beans and peas, fish and seafood, wholegrains and leafy greens (e.g. spinach). Low blood sugar can make you feel tired and so you must eat regularly to keep your blood sugar level **steady**. Don't skip meals and choose foods that **release** energy slowly, like proteins, wholegrains or nuts – try 30g of nuts a day.

You want to improve your mood

Serotonin is the 'happiness' hormone, so eat foods that help the body to make it, such as eggs or bananas – studies have shown that just four bananas a week can **cheer** you **up**! Also, make sure you're eating enough protein. The chemicals in protein are essential for the brain to **regulate** your feelings and thoughts. Good sources of protein are fish, eggs and legumes (peas, beans and lentils).

The longer read → Resource centre

3 Grammar

Modal verbs

1 Read the examples and answer the questions.

Talking about possibility
Eating the right foods can affect the way you feel.
The body can't get or make energy without B vitamins.

Talking about obligation/no obligation
You must eat regularly to keep your blood sugar level steady.
Normally, I have to have a snack or I have no energy.
You don't have to make many changes to have an impact.

Talking about prohibition
You mustn't eat more than 50g of dark chocolate.

1 Which modal(s) mean 'this is/isn't possible'?
2 Which modal(s) mean 'you are not allowed to do this'?
3 Which modal(s) mean 'it is necessary to do this'?
4 Which modal(s) mean 'this isn't necessary'?

Modals – third person singular
The modals have to/don't have to change for the third person (he, she, it). The other modals do not.
He doesn't have to study today.

2 Complete the sentences with the correct modal verb. There may be more than one possibility.

1 You (…) drink plenty of water to stay hydrated.
2 Eating mangoes (…) help you feel calm.
3 You (…) skip meals! It's really bad for you.
4 I (…) understand the text. It doesn't make sense.
5 Mark (…) study hard if he wants to pass the test.
6 You (…) come to the gym if you don't want to.

3 Read the examples. Complete the rules with past, specific or general.

Talking generally about the past
I could/was able to focus better.
Before, I couldn't/wasn't able to study without eating lots of sugary snacks.

Talking about a specific situation in the past
People were able to do better in memory tests using rosemary oil.
They couldn't/weren't able to focus in the exam.

Obligation and lack of obligation in the past
I had to rest because I had no energy.
Yesterday, I didn't have to buy any food for dinner.

1 When we talk about a (…) possibility in the past, we use could/couldn't or was/wasn't/were/weren't able to
2 When we talk about a (…) success in the past, we use was/were able to in the affirmative. However, in the negative, we can use either couldn't or wasn't/weren't able to.
3 When we talk about obligation in the (…) we use had to. When we talk about lack of obligation in the past we use didn't have to.

4 Choose the best answer.

The power of music

Research has shown that music 1 (…) lower blood pressure and reduce stress. Slow, calm music is best – you 2 (…) listen to classical music to relax, any calm music works! Singing along to songs 3 (…) also release tension and when hospital patients listened to music before and after surgery, they 4 (…) relax more and recovered faster. In another study, researchers found music 5 (…) increase self-esteem in older people. Headphones often increased the benefits – however, it is important to remember you 6 (…) turn the volume up too loud. Enjoy listening!

1	a must	b	can	c	had to
2	a don't have to	b	mustn't	c	couldn't
3	a has to	b	can't	c	can
4	a could	b	had to	c	was able to
5	a had to	b	could	c	must
6	a couldn't	b	mustn't	c	don't have to

5 Answer the question to solve the Brain teaser.

Artists can put a ship in a bottle – but can you think of a way to put a cucumber in a bottle?
1 You mustn't cut up the cucumber, it has to be whole.
2 You can't cut, change or break the bottle.
3 You don't have to do it quickly. Someone who was able to do it took two months.

How can you put a cucumber in a bottle?

6 Work in pairs. Complete the modal verb questions individually. Then ask and answer.

1 Were you (…) to do your last English homework?
2 (…) you understand exercise 4?
3 Did you (…) to get up early today?
4 (…) you usually focus for long periods?
5 (…) you speak English when you were a child?

Vocabulary and Listening 3

Phrasal verbs: healthy habits

1 Read the interview answers. Which things do you do too?

How do you stay *healthy*?

It's important to **take care of** yourself. I keep fit. I have an exercise routine and I **stick to** it! I spend time outdoors when I can. What else? I **talk through** any problems with my friends so I don't get stressed.

I **switch off** all my electronics for at least an hour before bed (really!). I try to go to bed and **get up** at the same time every day. That way, I get enough sleep and I **wake up** refreshed! I sometimes **stay up** late at the weekend, so I usually **sleep in** then.

I'm careful about what I eat and drink, but I don't always manage to have a healthy diet! I have **cut out** caffeine and fizzy drinks and I want to **cut down on** sugary snacks, especially before bed as they can keep me awake.

2 Read the interview answers again. Match the verbs in bold to the definitions 1–10.
1 continue sleeping after your alarm goes off
2 do something you decided you would do
3 turn off a piece of equipment
4 get out of bed
5 discuss
6 reduce
7 look after someone/something
8 stop eating or drinking something
9 stop sleeping
10 not go to bed

Transitive and intransitive phrasal verbs

Phrasal verbs can be transitive or intransitive.
Intransitive verbs don't need an object, e.g. *wake up*, *get up*.
I **get up** at 7 am. What time do you **wake up**?
Transitive verbs must have an object, e.g. *take care of* (someone/something), *talk through* (something).
Do you **take care of** yourself? Yes, I **take care of** myself.

3 Copy and complete the table with the verbs from the interviews.

Transitive	Intransitive
take care of	wake up

4 Complete the sentences with the correct phrasal verb. Then write sentences for the other verbs from exercise 3.
1 I'm not sure what to do. I'll (…) some ideas with my sister.
2 I'm putting my alarm on for 6 am because I want to (…) early.
3 We're going to a party tonight, so we'll (…) late!
4 She should (…) sugary snacks.
5 They don't have to get up early tomorrow. They can (…) until 9 am!

5 💬 Work in pairs. Discuss the questions.
1 How many hours' sleep do you get?
2 Do you have a routine before bed?
3 What can you do to get a good night's sleep?

A conversation

6 🔊 19 Listen to Jake and Erin's conversation. Which topic in exercise 5 do they not discuss?

▶ **Subskill: Recognising informal speech**

In informal speech we often use: contractions; shorter sentences; informal expressions; clarification; abbreviations; phrasal verbs.

7 Read the extract from the conversation. How many features of informal speech can you find?

> I didn't stay up late. I just couldn't get to sleep. I mean, I was awake for ages, you know?

8 Listen again. Are the statements true or false? Correct the false statements.
1 Not many experts think teenagers should start school later.
2 Jake usually feels tired at about 10 pm.
3 Teenagers should sleep eight to ten hours a night.
4 Scientists say school should start at 8.30 am at the earliest.
5 It's a good idea to switch off electronics at least three hours before bed.
6 You shouldn't have sugary snacks or fizzy drinks before bed.

9 💬 Work in pairs. Ask and answer the questions.
1 Who do you talk your problems through with?
2 Do you get enough sleep? What could you do to improve it?
3 Would you like to start school later? Why/Why not?

41

3 Grammar

Gerund and infinitive

1 Read the examples. Then match sentences a–f to rules 1–6.

> a It's hard to think if you haven't slept enough.
> b Starting school later helps prevent accidents.
> c The experts suggested starting school later.
> d Teens need to sleep eight to ten hours a night.
> e Use thick curtains to stop the light coming in.
> f I'm interested in finding out more.

We use the gerund …
1 after certain verbs (e.g. *enjoy*, *suggest*, *finish*)
2 as the subject of a sentence
3 after prepositions

We use the infinitive …
4 after certain verbs (e.g. *want*, *decide*, *need*)
5 to talk about purpose
6 after adjectives (e.g. *necessary*, *easy*, *delighted*)

Gerund or infinitive?

Some verbs can take either the gerund or the infinitive with no change of meaning, e.g. *like, love, hate, can't stand, prefer, continue*. Using the gerund is more common.

I like watching films. / I like to watch films.
She continued talking. / She continued to talk.

However, when we talk about the future or imagine something, we use *would* + verb + infinitive.

I would like to go to Canada one day.

2 Choose the correct option. Look at the rules and give reasons for your answers.
1 I go to bed at 9 pm **to get**/**getting** enough sleep.
2 It's important **to drink**/**drinking** plenty of water.
3 **To spend**/**Spending** time outdoors is healthy.
4 I'm interested in **to do**/**doing** more exercise.
5 Karen exercises by **to cycle**/**cycling** every day.

3 Copy and complete the table with the verbs in the box. Add any others you know.

> admit   agree   can't stand   choose   plan   hope
> learn   miss   offer   practise   prefer   promise

Verb + infinitive	Verb + gerund	Verb + infinitive or gerund
decide, need, want	enjoy	like

4 Complete the sentences with the correct form of the verbs. Write four sentences of your own.
1 Mark admitted (…) **(lose)** the sports equipment.
2 I want (…) **(go)** swimming later.
3 Will can't stand (…) **(listen)** to people talking about food!
4 They promised (…) **(eat)** healthy snacks.
5 I'm planning (…) **(download)** that new health app.
6 You missed (…) **(see)** a great documentary.

5 Complete the text with the correct form of the verbs in brackets.

Exercise – happy body, happy mind

Exercise isn't just good for your body, it's good for your mind too. **1** (…) **(exercise)** regularly helps with stress, mood and sleep! When you learn **2** (…) **(play)** a sport and succeed, it's also good for your self-esteem. Many teenagers choose **3** (…) **(do)** team sports because spending time with others makes them happier. It isn't always easy **4** (…) **(fit)** exercise into a busy day, so experts recommend **5** (…) **(make)** it part of your daily routine – for example by **6** (…) **(walk)** or cycling to school. They also suggest **7** (…) **(do)** some exercise outdoors as sunlight contains vitamin D, which lifts your mood.

6 Choose the correct option.

GRAMMAR ROUND-UP
1 2 3 **4 5 6 7 8**

Let's talk

Anxiety can be a common problem, but most young people don't like **1 talk/talking** about it. YouTube star Zoe Sugg, hopes **2 to change/changing** that. Zoe **3 has/is having** a vlog called Zoella with over 8 million followers. She usually talks about beauty, fashion and life, but she **4 was using/has used** her vlog to talk about her own experiences of panic attacks and anxiety too. That's why the charity Mind **5 chose/has chosen** her as its Digital Ambassador. Zoe launched their new campaign #Don'tPanicButton. People wear the button if they suffer from anxiety or if they want **6 to show/showing** their support for others. Then they post photos of themselves online wearing the badge. Both Zoe and the organisers think digital media **7 must/can** help young people and increase awareness of problems like this by **8 to show/showing** them they are not alone – and that it's OK to talk about what they feel.

Real-world speaking 3

Per person:
1 cup of almond milk
1 banana
fresh strawberries, 1 peach
¼ cup of oats
½ teaspoon of cinnamon
1 tablespoon of honey

Giving instructions

1 Look at the photos and ingredients. What do you think Katya is learning to make?

2 🎥 Watch the video. In what order does Malik mention the ingredients?

Katya
I really enjoyed the gym today … but now I'm hungry and thirsty!

Malik
Why don't we make some smoothies? They only take **1** (…) minutes to make.

Katya
Cool. So what do we have to do?

Malik
First, get the ingredients. You can add any fruit … let's see, we have some strawberries, **2** (…) peaches and two bananas – perfect for two!

Katya
What's next?

Malik
Chop the fruit, and I'll get the milk and the other ingredients.

Katya
Like this? Is that OK or should I do them smaller?

Malik
No, that's great. OK, put all the fruit into the blender.

Katya
Sure, what now?

Malik
Then add **3** (…) cups of milk, **4** (…) tablespoon of honey, and half a cup of oats. I add the oats if I'm hungry. And last, one teaspoon of cinnamon … that's for flavor.

Katya
OK, I've done that. Shall I mix it now?

Malik
Yeah, but you have to put the lid on! OK, turn on the blender now for **5** (…) seconds or so.

Katya
I nearly forgot the lid! And now?

Malik
Pour it into two glasses. Then all you have to do is drink it!

3 Watch again and complete the dialogue with the correct numbers.

4 Read the Key phrases. Which preparing food verbs are in the dialogue?

5 Create your own dialogue. Follow the steps in the Skills boost.

SKILLS BOOST

THINK
Choose a healthy recipe. Make notes of the ingredients and instructions. Find a photo or photos.

PREPARE
Prepare a dialogue. Remember to include phrases for preparing food and sequencing.

PRACTISE
Practise your dialogue.

PERFORM
Act out your dialogue for the class.

6 Peer review Listen to your classmates. Answer the questions.
  1 What do they make?
  2 Which Key phrases do they use?
  3 Could they improve their dialogue? How?

Key phrases

Sequencing
First … Next … Then … Finally

Preparing food
Get/Measure/Add the ingredients.
Cut/Chop (it/them/the fruit) into pieces.
Mix/Cook (it/them/the dish) for (2 minutes).
Pour (it/the mix/the liquid) into (a glass/a pan).
A/One cup/teaspoon/tablespoon/handful of (fruit).

🇺🇸💬 US → UK 🇬🇧

flavor (US) → flavour (UK)

3 Writing

Rosa Gonzalez To: Nico Blanco 11/02 18:50 Attachments 1MB

Fun Run!

Hi Nico,

How are you doing? Sorry I haven't written for ages, I've been really busy at school. Guess what? It's our school's health week soon. My class had to organise an event, so we decided to have a Fun Run in our local park. It's only five kilometres, and you don't have to run; you can walk, skip or skateboard round the course instead. It costs £5.00 to enter, but the money goes to SportsAid (a charity for young athletes). The Fun Run's on 20th February and it starts at 10.30 am. Anyone can come!! It'll be great fun and you're always saying you want to keep fit and spend time outdoors! Please, please come! Mum says you can stay for the weekend if you want, so we can meet up with my friends in the evening.

I can't wait to hear all your news. What have you been doing? What about your family and friends, are they all OK? Write soon!

Love

Rosa

P.S. Text me when you know if you're coming or not. I have to register you for the event.

An informal email

1 Work in pairs. Does your school organise any events to promote sports and other healthy activities?

2 Read the email quickly and answer the questions.
1. What is the event?
2. Who can take part?
3. Where and when is it?
4. How much does it cost?

▶ **Subskill: Using punctuation**

Punctuation is necessary for our writing to make sense. Punctuation marks include: exclamation mark **!** question mark **?** comma **,** apostrophe **'** brackets **( )** full stop **.**

3 Read the email again and find an example of each type of punctuation in the information about punctuation. Which is used:
1. to finish a sentence?
2. after a question?
3. at the end of a sentence to show surprise, excitement or other strong emotions?
4. to separate items in a list or separate two clauses?
5. in contractions and possessive forms?
6. to separate extra information from the rest of the sentence?

4 Add punctuation to the following sentences.
1. Students friends and families are welcome
2. Can you come to the event
3. Zumba is a fun energetic activity and you dont need any experience
4. Feel the music and get dancing
5. As part of Health Week were organising a Zumba Dance Party
6. Health Week aims to get people active in a fun easy way

5 Write an email to invite a friend to come to another event during Health Week. Follow the steps in the Skills boost.

SKILLS BOOST

THINK
Decide on an event. Choose from the events below or think of an event of your own.
- Zumba Dance Party
- Making healthy snacks
- Sponsored walk or swim
- Bike ride

Make notes of all the information you need to include. Include answers to all the questions in exercise 2.

PREPARE
Organise your notes. Where are you going to put each piece of information?
Find the photos or images that you need.

WRITE
Write the email. Use the model and your notes to help you.

CHECK
Read your email. Answer the questions.
1 Have you used the correct punctuation?
2 Have you used modal verbs?
3 Have you used gerunds and infinitives correctly?
4 Have you included health vocabulary?

6 **Peer review** Exchange your email with another student. Answer the questions.
1 Read your partner's email. What event is it for? Has he/she included the answers to the questions in exercise 2?
2 Has your partner included all the things in the checklist?
3 Would you like to go to the event? Why/Why not?

QUICK REVIEW 3

Grammar

Modal verbs
We can use modals to express possibility, obligation, and prohibition.
Anyone **can** take part in the Fun Run.
You **can't** get fit if you don't exercise.
You **must** register for the event.
I **have to** help organise the day.
You **don't have to** run, you can walk instead.
You **mustn't** forget to bring some music.

Past modal verbs
We **could** / **were able to** do all the dances.
They **couldn't** / **weren't able to** use the school hall.
The Fun Run was hard, but I **was able to** finish it.
I **couldn't** / **wasn't able to** get to the end.
We **had to** organise an event.
I **didn't have to** pay any money.

Gerund and infinitive
We use the gerund …
1 after certain verbs
   The experts **suggested starting** school earlier.
2 as the subject of a sentence
   Eating the right food can affect the way you feel.
3 after prepositions
   She is very good **at playing** the piano.

We use the infinitive …
1 after certain verbs
   I **decided to cut down on** sugary snacks.
2 to talk about purpose
   Go to bed earlier **to get** a good night's sleep.
3 after certain adjectives
   It's **hard** for teenagers **to feel** tired before 11pm.

Vocabulary

🔊 20 Staying healthy
do exercise, eat fruit and vegetables, eat less sugar, have a healthy diet, play sports, watch less TV

🔊 21 Health and well-being
drink enough water, eat fast food, eat too quickly, have sugary snacks, feel stressed, get active, get enough sleep, go to bed late, improve your mood, keep fit, skip breakfast, spend time outdoors

🔊 22 Phrasal verbs: healthy habits
cut down on, cut out, get up, sleep in, stay up, stick to, switch off, take care of, talk through, wake up

45

Project

How can you improve your health?

TASK: Plan a fitness weekend and create a diary to show how successfully you carried it out.

Learning outcomes
1. I can work with classmates to plan a fitness diary for a weekend.
2. I can evaluate different ideas.
3. I can use appropriate language from the unit.

Graphic organiser → Project planner p119

1 Watch a video of students presenting a diary of their fitness weekend. Answer the questions.
1. How many activities did the group do each day?
2. Did they need any equipment for the activities?

STEP 1: THINK

2 Look at the fitness weekend diary in the Model project. Answer the questions.
1. Why did the group choose cycling?
2. Why was walking an easy activity to plan?
3. Why was the weekend great? Give three reasons.

STEP 2: PLAN

3 Work in groups of three. Read the tips in the Super skills box and practise saying the Key phrases with your group.

CREATIVITY

Evaluating different ideas

Tips
Think of as many ideas as you can.
Discuss the advantages and disadvantages of each idea.
Choose the best idea or ideas.

Key phrases
What (else) do we have to do?
The first thing to do is … Then … Next …
I think (cycling) is better/more fun/easier than (climbing) because …
(Volleyball) isn't as easy to arrange as (walking) because …
Do you agree/think (cycling) is the best option?
Have we reached a final decision?

4 Make your fitness plan in your groups. Use the tips and Key phrases in the Super skills box.

STEP 3: CREATE

5 Look at the ways of making a record of your fitness diary. Answer the questions.

| photo story | comic | report | video |

1. Which one do you prefer? Why?
2. How else could you make a record of what you did?

6 Read the *How to …* tips on p119. Make sure you have everything you need to do the fitness activities and record them. Then carry out the activities.

7 Create your fitness diary. Record what you did each day and how you got on.

46   Grammar and Vocabulary → Quick review p45

Model project

Saturday
We got up early and met in the park. We cycled for an hour to get fit! We had to bring our bikes and helmets and wear suitable clothes. We chose cycling because it's a great way of exercising outdoors.

We made sure we drank enough water 😃.

Sunday morning
We went skateboarding. Max fell off but he didn't stop trying.

Sunday afternoon
We went for a walk. We didn't have to take any equipment so it was an easy activity to plan. We loved spending time outdoors together.

Our weekend was great! We stuck to our plan, got active and we switched off all electronics for a few hours. Taking care of ourselves was fun!

Emma was able to learn a new trick! Yay!

STEP 4: PRESENT

8 Show your fitness diary to the class.

9 **Peer review** Answer your classmates' questions about it.

3 FINAL REFLECTION

1 **The task**
How successful was your fitness diary?
How easy was it to produce?

2 **Super skills**
How well did you evaluate different ideas?

3 **Language**
What new language from this unit did you use? Give examples.

Beyond the task
Why is it important to have healthy habits? What do *you* want to change about your health habits?

4 Invention

WDYT? (What do you think?)

What makes a good invention? What's the best way to present it to people?

Vocabulary: jobs in science; science; describing products; negative prefixes

Grammar: past perfect; relative pronouns; defining relative clauses

Reading: an online article about science making a difference

Listening: a talk on an invention

Speaking: checking information

Writing: a formal letter

Project: a product pitch

Video skills p49

Real-world speaking p55

Project pp58–59

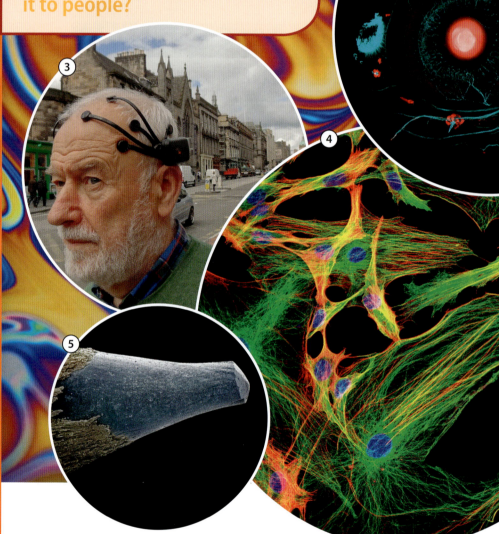

Jobs in science

1 Work in pairs. Look at the jobs. Add any more jobs you can think of and then decide which job is the most interesting. Why?

> biologist   chemist   doctor   engineer   entrepreneur
> inventor   physicist   researcher   scientist

2 Copy and complete the table with the jobs from exercise 1.

-er / -eer	-or	-ist	other spelling
engineer	inventor	scientist	entrepreneur

48

Vocabulary 4

a How can you write or draw and rub it out? A scientist **came up with** the solution in 1795 by putting graphite between two pieces of wood. Engineers have **developed** this product to make the popular modern pencil. That's how they **invented** it!

b Believe it or not, this is part of a mouse's brain! A biologist took the picture when she was **investigating** vision and how the brain works. She hopes to **make** some exciting discoveries.

c This is actually a soap bubble in water. The image was taken when scientists were **researching** how foam is made by drinks and washing up liquid.

d Imagine wearing this! Researchers **created** this invention to record brain activity. They **designed** the device to fit on someone's head. They were **doing** research to see how people's feelings change when they go to different places.

e It might look like modern art, but it's a fish's eye. The Zebrafish's eye responds to movement in water and scientists are hoping to **discover** how it does this They are **doing** experiments to find out.

Verb and noun collocations: science

3 Look at photos 1–5. What do you think these things are? Use your imagination!

4 In pairs, match photos 1–5 to descriptions a–e.

5 Read the texts again. Which verb goes with which noun in the texts? Match the verbs with the nouns in the boxes.

Verbs

create   come up with   design   develop   discover
do x2   invent   investigate   make   research

Nouns

a device   a discovery   an experiment   an invention
a product x2   research   a solution   something x3

6 Work in pairs. Choose the correct words and answer the questions. Then write 3–5 more questions and exchange with another pair.

How much do you know about science?

1 Who **invented/discovered** the mobile phone?
2 Who **created/investigated** the radio?
3 Who **discovered/developed** radium and polonium?
4 Who **made/came up with** the idea of the Internet?
5 Who **developed/did** early computer codes?
6 Who **discovered/invented** penicillin?

Martin Cooper   Marie Curie
Alexander Fleming   Tim Berners-Lee
Ada Lovelace   Guglielmo Marconi

7 Work in pairs. Discuss which things you would most like to do. Give reasons for your answers.

discover a new planet • design a device to save lives • investigate a disease to find a cure • develop a best-selling product • invent a product to reduce pollution • research alternatives to plastic • come up with a solution for a serious problem

VIDEO SKILLS

8 Watch the video with no sound. What do you think it is about?

9 Watch the video with sound. Were your answers to 8 correct?

10 Work in pairs. Discuss the questions.
1 What have you learnt from the video?
2 Which typical features of a documentary were in the video? How did they give us more information about the topic?
  a interviews   **b** voiceover
  c footage of real-life events

Pronunciation: diphthongs → p116

49

4 Reading and critical thinking

An online article

1 What vocabulary do you remember? Copy and complete the table.

People in science	Things they do
scientist, engineer …	invent a product, research …

2 🔊 23 Look at the photos and the title of the text. Which words from exercise 1 do you think will be in the text? Read and check your answers.

▶ **Subskill: Identifying text purpose**

To help you understand the purpose of a text, think about: Where is the text from? Who is it for? Why was it written?

3 Read the subskill information. Then read the text again and answer the questions. Give evidence to support your answer.

1 The text is probably from
   a a popular science website
   b an online science textbook
2 The text is probably for
   a researchers at university
   b people who are interested in science
3 What is the writer's purpose?
   a To instruct people in building an invention.
   b To inform scientists about new research and inventions.
   c To encourage young people to invent things.
   d To advise people how to be successful inventors.

4 Read the sentences and write Eesha, Anurudh or both.
1 She/He has personal experience of the problem.
2 She/He loved science when she/he was younger.
3 Her/His invention could be used with many different types of device.
4 She/He won something because of the invention.
5 She/He found a solution to the problem she/he wanted to solve.
6 Her/His invention can also help people who need power at home.

5 Complete the sentences.
1 Eesha's device can charge a phone …
2 You can use a 'supercapacitor' with …
3 Eesha designed the materials …
4 Vaccines are important because …
5 Anurudh couldn't have the vaccine because …
6 The fridge stays cool when …

6 **Word work** Find the words in the box in the text. Can you guess the meaning? Match the words with the definitions.

| charge   generate   healthcare |
| improve   remote   trailer |

1 far away from other cities, towns or people
2 produce power
3 make something better
4 the services that look after people's health
5 put electricity into a battery
6 something you can attach to a vehicle to move things

7 Complete the sentences with the words from exercise 6.
1 I think the best way to (…) electricity is solar energy.
2 It isn't necessary to (…) most devices like mobiles. They're fine as they are.
3 I don't like cities. I'd like to live in a (…) village.
4 You should (…) your phone every day, so that you'll always have power.
5 It isn't the government's responsibility to provide (…) . People should pay to see a doctor.
6 All cars should come with a (…) . Then you could transport more things easily.

8 💬 Work in pairs. Do you agree or disagree with the sentences in exercise 7? Discuss.

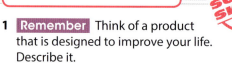

CRITICAL THINKING

1 **Remember** Think of a product that is designed to improve your life. Describe it.
2 **Analyse** Make a list of its strengths and weaknesses and evaluate it. Think about this: Is it practical? Is it good value for money?
3 **Evaluate** Explain how the product could be improved.

Research

Find out about how an object you use every day was invented. Could the object be improved? How?

Science making a difference

Could you invent something that makes the world a better place? These two young people did that, and you could too! Find out what inspired them and how they did it.

Has your phone battery ever run out just when you needed to use it? Well, that could soon be a thing of the past! Eesha Khare, a young American engineer, has invented a device that could **charge** a phone in just 20–30 seconds! Not only that, but you'd have battery power for far longer. It's called a 'supercapacitor' and it could be used for any electronic device, even cars. For her device, Eesha used materials that she had designed at the University of California. Eesha had always loved chemistry so it's no surprise she wanted to **improve** technology using it. Eesha's device isn't just good news for tech-loving teenagers. It could help millions in countries where not everyone has electricity at home – not just to charge phones, but perhaps fridges, cookers and lights too. Eesha won a $50,000 science prize for her invention.

Anurudh Ganesan created a simple, safe way to transport vaccines to **remote** health clinics. Vaccines protect people from diseases and save millions of lives every year. In some countries, health workers have to take vaccines long distances by bike or even on foot in containers with ice. If the vaccines get too warm, they don't work.

Anurudh lives in the USA, but he was born in India. When he was a baby, his grandparents took him to a health clinic. When they arrived, however, they found the vaccines there were all useless. The ice that kept the vaccinations cool had melted before the health worker reached the clinic. It was a common problem.

When Anurudh was 15, he wanted to find a solution. He designed a trailer with a fridge on it – the Vaxxwagon. It uses movement instead of electricity to keep the fridge cool. When someone pulls the **trailer**, the wheels turn and **generate** power.

His invention has already won an international science prize and now Anurudh's dream is to create better **healthcare** worldwide.

So, what are you waiting for? Your invention could be the next big thing!

4 Grammar

Past perfect

1 Read the examples, look at the timelines and choose the correct option in the rules.

> After she had come up with the idea, she was able to develop the device.
> The ice had melted before the health worker reached the clinic.
> Anurudh hadn't designed anything before he created his invention.
> Had Eesha done any research before she created the device?

First action	Second action	→ Now
She came up with the idea	She developed the device	
The ice melted	The health worker reached the clinic	

1 We use the past perfect to talk about actions or situations that happened **before/after** a specific time or another action in the past. We use it to make it clear which action happened first.

2 The past perfect clause **can/can't** come first or second in the sentence. The order isn't important.

3 We **can/can't** use the short forms 'd (had) and hadn't (had not).

> **after, before, when, by**
> After she had done a lot of research, she had an idea.
> She had worked for months before she found a solution.
> She had just bought the materials when I saw her.
> By the time I arrived, they had already tried lots of ideas.

2 Complete the sentences. Use contractions where possible.

1 We (…) **(try)** different things before we found a solution.
2 After she (…) **(invent)** a new machine, she won a prize.
3 The class (…) **(just/start)** when we got to the science laboratory.
4 When I saw him, Mark (…) **(not finish)** his experiment.
5 (…) **(they/create)** any inventions before they invented this product?
6 Before I chose this one, I (…) **(already/test)** a lot of other products.

3 Choose the correct options.

Who invented crisps?

In 1853, George Crum was cooking in a restaurant in Saratoga Springs. When he found out that a customer **1 complained/ had complained** about his chips, Crum **2 decided/had decided** to cut the potatoes thinner. The customer **3 complained/had complained** again. By this time, Crum **4 had/had had** enough! After he **5 cut/had cut** the potatoes as thin as he could, he **6 cooked/had cooked** them in hot oil. The customer **7 loved/had loved** them – and Crum **8 invented/had invented** crisps!

4 Write questions using the past perfect or past simple. Then answer the questions.

1 who / complain / about the chips ?
2 the customer / complain again ?
3 why / Crum / have enough ?
4 how / Crum / cook the really thin potatoes ?
5 what / he / invent ?

5 Complete the text with the past perfect or past simple form of the verbs in brackets.

A tasty invention

In 1937, Ruth Wakefield and her husband owned a hotel and restaurant in America and Ruth 1 (…) (cook) for the guests. One day while she was making cookies she 2 (…) (realise) that she 3 (…) (run out) of cooking chocolate. She 4 (…) (forget) to buy it! Ruth 5 (…) (decide) to use normal chocolate instead. She chopped a bar into small pieces and hoped the pieces would melt. When she 6 (…) (take) the cookies out of the oven, she discovered the chocolate 7 (…) (not melt) . By accident, Ruth 8 (…) (invent) the chocolate chip cookie!

6 Answer the questions to solve the Brain teaser.

John, Ruth, Sami, Tobias and Kiera were working on different inventions.

1 John hadn't finished when the first invention was ready.
2 Tobias had done his research before Kiera, but she developed her invention before him.
3 Sami finished her invention after John.
4 Ruth had created an invention before Tobias, but then she had a problem. She finished after he'd produced his final version.
5 John wasn't the last to finish; three others had finished before him.

Who finished first? In what order did they finish?

Vocabulary and Listening 4

Describing products

1 Look at the photos of two products and answer the questions.
1. What do you think they are?
2. How would you describe them? What adjectives could you use? Write notes.

2 Read the reviews and match the descriptions to the photos. Then answer the questions.
1. Did you guess correctly the answer to question 1 in exercise 1?
2. Do the reviews use any of the adjectives you wrote in question 2?

★★★★★
1 The FITT360 is a **wearable** camera that records 360° images. It's also a **wireless** headset for music or phone calls. It's **comfortable** and **easy to use** and the images are **high quality**. It's **practical** too because you don't need to use your hands to record. It costs around $150.   Gary16

★★★★
2 Play your music with this **innovative** wireless speaker. It's **handy** because it's also a lamp that changes colour when you touch it, with 6 different colours to choose from. It's a **useful** gadget and at around $20 it isn't **expensive**. It's **well made** and **reliable**.   TechRachel

3 Match six of the words or phrases in bold with the definitions.
1. technology that communicates using electronic signals
2. useful
3. new, original and advanced
4. intended to be useful, not just look good
5. you can carry it on the body
6. very good or excellent standard

4 Match the adjectives to their opposites in exercise 2. Which ones use negative prefixes? How do you form the other ones?

badly made	cheap	hard to use
impractical	inexpensive	low quality
uncomfortable	unreliable	useless

A talk

5 Read the questions and check the meaning of the words in bold. Then look at the photo and answer the questions.
1. What do you think the product is?
2. What do you think the **packaging** is made from?
3. Do you think it **harms** the **environment**?
4. Which words could you use to describe this product?

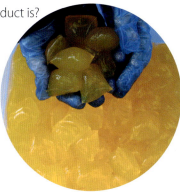

6 🔊 24 Listen to Lidia's talk and check your guesses.

▶ **Subskill: Listening for the information you need**

In gapped sentences, read the sentences and decide if you need a name, a number, a date, an adjective, etc.

7 Read the sentences and decide what information you need. Listen again and complete the sentences.
1. Around (…) % of plastic bottles are recycled.
2. Every year, between five and (…) tonnes of plastic bottles end up in the ocean.
3. An Ooho is a small round (…) with a 'skin' you can eat.
4. Oohos don't (…) so they are very practical.
5. The inventors have (…) the product out in London.
6. (…) of people watched a video on YouTube.

8 Read the sentences. Are they true, false or is there no information? Listen and check.
1. Most recycled plastic bottles are used to make new bottles.
2. Skipping Rocks Lab want to produce alternatives to plastic bottles, cups and plates.
3. It takes a long time to make the packaging to hold the water.
4. Making Oohos is cheaper than making plastic bottles for water.
5. You can buy Oohos in shops in London.
6. It is possible to make Oohos at home quite easily.

9 💬 Work in pairs. Discuss the questions.
1. Would you buy an Ooho? Why/Why not?
2. What other ways do you know of avoiding plastic bottles?

53

4 Grammar

Relative pronouns

1 Read the examples and complete the rules.

> **Relative pronouns**
> London is the city **where** the company is based.
> It's a company **which/that** aims to produce alternatives to plastic bottles.
> People **who/that** have tried them say you don't taste the skin.
> He's the man **whose** idea it was.
> Will there ever be a day **when** we don't use plastic?

1 We use relative pronouns to refer to nouns. We use:
  a (…) and (…) to talk about people
  b (…) and (…) to talk about things
  c (…) to talk about places
  d (…) to talk about time
  e (…) to talk about possession
2 The relative pronouns come **before/after** the noun.

2 Choose the correct options for descriptions 1–6. Then match them to the words in the box.

> 1942   Stephen Hawking   the UK   his daughter
> time, space and black holes   Barack Obama

FACT FILE:

1 a scientist **who/whose** book *A Brief History of Time* has sold millions of copies and **who/which** was famous for his research
2 the country **where/which** he was born
3 the year **which/when** he was born (he died in 2018)
4 the President of the United States **that/whose** gave Stephen Hawking a medal
5 the person **who/which** he wrote a book with
6 the subjects **where/which** most fascinated him

Defining relative clauses

3 Look at the examples and choose the correct option.

> **Defining relative clauses**
> They have tested it out in London. That's **the city where they're based**.
> Some of **the people who watched the online video** made their own videos.

1 We **can/can't** use defining relative clauses to give essential information about someone or something.
2 We **need/don't need** this information to understand who or what we are talking about. The sentence doesn't make sense without it.
3 The clause **usually/never** comes immediately after the noun it refers to.

4 Join the sentences using defining relative clauses. Make any necessary changes.
1 Alexander Graham Bell is the man. He invented the telephone.
2 Bell moved from Scotland to Canada. He started his experiments there.
3 He was investigating sound in 1879. He discovered a way to communicate over distance.
4 He used a magnet. It turned sound into electricity.
5 Bell is the man. His invention changed the way we communicate.

5 Complete the text with one word in each gap.

> **GRAMMAR ROUND-UP**
> 1 2 3 4 **5 6 7 8**
>
> A 16-year-old called George Nissen invented the trampoline in 1934. Nissen **1** (…) an athlete **2** (…) loved gymnastics. He **3** (…) recently watched some acrobats at a circus. While they **4** (…) performing, they used a safety net. This inspired him to build an invention which he **5** (…) bounce up and down on. Nissen called his invention the 'trampoline'. After improving the design, Nissen started a company **6** (…) produced trampolines. He demonstrated his invention all over the country and at one demonstration he performed with a kangaroo. A photo of the event appeared in newspapers around the world and the trampoline **7** (…) popular worldwide. In 2000 trampolining became an Olympic event. **8** (…) then, trampoline parks have opened all over the world.

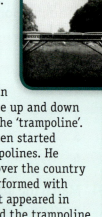

Checking information

1 Look at the photos. Have you been to see a light show?

2 📹 Watch the video. What do Joe and Kate agree about the following?
 1 the time to go   2 what to eat

3 Watch again. Then complete the dialogue with the words in the box.

> do we   don't you   wasn't there   weren't there

Joe: I'm really excited about this light show.
Kate: Me too. It starts at 6:00 pm, doesn't it?
Joe: Yeah, that's right. So we can go at 6:00 pm and spend two hours at the show.
Kate: But there was a lot to see last time, 1 (…) ?
Joe: That's true. OK, so what about food?
Kate: There were a lot of cafés 2 (…) ?
Joe: Yes, but we didn't eat there last time, did we? Remember? It was too expensive.
Kate: OK. Let's take a sandwich and some snacks. We don't have to buy tickets, 3 (…) ?
Joe: No, it's free.
Kate: There is a bus stop nearby, isn't there?
Joe: Yeah, I checked. You want to go, 4 (…) ?
Kate: Yes, of course. Why?
Joe: You're asking a lot of questions!

Real-world speaking 4

4 Watch again. Which two Key phrases aren't in the dialogue?

5 Create your own dialogue. Follow the steps in the Skills boost.

SKILLS BOOST

THINK
Choose an event that you and your partner would like to go to. Decide on the following and make notes.
- What time to meet
- How to get there
- Where/What to eat

PREPARE
Prepare a dialogue. Remember to include phrases for checking the information.

PRACTISE
Practise your dialogue. Remember to use correct intonation in question tags.

PERFORM
Act out your dialogue for the class.

6 **Peer review** Listen to your classmates. Answer the questions.
 1 Which event do they go to?
 2 Which Key phrases do they use?

Key phrases

Checking about the present:
The light show starts at 6:00 pm, <u>doesn't it?</u>↑
We don't have to buy tickets, <u>do we?</u>↑
It's on for four nights, <u>isn't it?</u>↑

Checking about the past:
You checked the route, <u>didn't you?</u>↑
We didn't eat there last time, <u>did we?</u>↑
There was a lot to see last time, <u>wasn't there?</u>↑
There were a lot of cafés, <u>weren't there?</u>↑

Phrasebook → p123   55

4 Writing

A

SCIENCE TODAY

Calling all inventors! Send us an article about your invention and we will publish the best ones. The writer of the winning article will appear on a radio show to present their invention. Articles should include photos.

Send your article to: The Editor, Science Today, 15 Green Road, London PR3 2JLB

B

BCT Television are looking for candidates for our new show *Entrepreneur*.

Are you 16–24 years old? Have you invented something? Would you like to develop and sell your product? Could you present it to a group of experts to win funding? If so, contact us now! This is an exciting opportunity to make your dream come true.

Send your CV and covering letter to: Applications department, *Entrepreneur*, BCT Television, 55 Stone Street, London, NW1 3BG

---

[a] 32 Windsor Road
Manchester M22 4TN
[b] Tel: 07988 392239
l.stokes33@mail.com

[c] Applications department
Entrepreneur
BCT Television
55 Stone Street
London NW1 3BG

[d] 02 December, 2020

[e] Dear Sir or Madam,

[f] **I am writing** to apply to appear on your television show *Entrepreneur*! I feel strongly that my innovative new product will be of interest. It is an easy-to-use device which can significantly increase Internet speed. It is well made and reliable.

I enclose my CV and photos of my invention. As you will see, I already have some experience in giving presentations. In addition, last summer I worked in a laboratory where I got useful experience of developing new products. Furthermore, I recently took part in a workshop for young designers which helped me improve my invention. I am sure that you will agree that it is a high-quality, practical device that viewers will enjoy learning about.

Thank you for considering my application. **I would be happy to** attend an interview at any time. **Please contact me on** the number or email address given above if you require any further information. **I look forward to** hearing from you.

[e] Yours faithfully,

[g] *Lexie Stokes*
Lexie Stokes

A formal letter

1 Read the two adverts and the letter and answer the questions.
  1 Which advert is the letter for?
  2 Has the writer got any experience of presenting?
  3 What does Lexie's product do?

2 Match 1–7 with a–g in the letter.
  1 Write the date.
  2 Sign the letter and type your name below it.
  3 Write *Dear Sir or Madam* and finish *Yours faithfully*. If you know the name, write *Dear (Name)* and finish *Yours sincerely*.
  4 Include your contact details.
  5 Write your address on the right.
  6 Write the other person's title and the address.
  7 Write the main part of the letter.

▶ **Subskill: Using formal language**
We use formal language to express what we need to say politely, e.g. *I am writing to …, I enclose …, Thank you for considering …, I would be happy to …, Please contact me on …, I look forward to …*

3 Read the letter again and match the phrases in bold to 1–6. Which phrase is used to …
  1 ask the person to phone or email you?
  2 explain the reason you are writing?
  3 say what you could do?
  4 politely thank someone for reading the letter?
  5 politely say you would like them to respond?
  6 say what you are including with the letter?

4 Complete the sentences with one of the phrases in bold.
  1 (…) my article. I hope you agree it is interesting for readers.
  2 (…) hearing from you in the near future.
  3 (…) in response to your advert.
  4 (…) answer any questions you may have about my invention.
  5 (…) my mobile, 07944 56789.
  6 (…) my article and some photos of my invention.

5 Add two more expressions from the letter to each box.

Introducing an opinion	Adding information
In my view	*Also*

56

6 Complete the sentences using relative pronouns.
1 My invention is a pack (…) contains LED strips.
2 These are strips (…) you can cut to any length and attach to clothes.
3 People (…) buy the LED strips can create their own costumes.
4 This would be great for times (…) you go camping with friends.
5 A person (…) wears one of these costumes is easy to see at night, so they can stay safe on the roads.
6 This is an exciting new product (…) will be popular with teenagers.

7 Write a letter to respond to advert B in exercise 1. Follow the steps in the Skills boost.

THINK
Think of an invention or use the invention from exercise 6. Write notes to describe it.

PREPARE
Organise your notes into paragraphs:
Paragraph 1: say why you're writing and give a brief description of the product
Paragraph 2: give details to support your application
Paragraph 3: close the letter and politely ask for action

WRITE
Write your letter. Use the model letter to help you.

CHECK
Read your letter. Answer the questions.
1 Have you organised your letter into paragraphs?
2 Have you used formal expressions?
3 Have you used relative pronouns and relative clauses?
4 Have you included science vocabulary and vocabulary for describing inventions?

8 Peer review Exchange your letter with another student. Answer the questions.
1 Is the letter well organised?
2 Does the letter make you want to find out more about the invention?

QUICK REVIEW

Grammar

Past perfect
We use the past perfect to talk about actions or situations that happened before a specific time or another action in the past. We use it to make clear which action happened first.
*We used strips that **had** already **been** cut to size.*
*They **had finished** the presentation before we arrived.*
***Had** the inventors **developed** another product before this one?*

Relative pronouns
We use relative pronouns to talk about nouns.
We use *who* and *that* to talk about people.
*People **who/that** buy the strips can create their own costumes.*
We use *which* and *that* to talk about things.
*It's a product **which/that** will be popular with teens.*
We use *where* to talk about places.
*They can be used in places **where** there isn't much light.*
We use *when* to talk about time.
*They're useful at night **when** it's dark.*
We use *whose* to talk about possession.
*People **whose** costumes use the lights love them.*

Defining relative clauses
*Eesha is the girl **who/that** invented that new device.*
*It's a device **which/that** can charge phones quickly.*
*Inventors are people **whose** job it is to create new designs.*
*It was a year **when** many new things were invented.*
*London was the city **where** the inventor was born.*

Vocabulary

🔊 25 Jobs in science
biologist, chemist, doctor, engineer, entrepreneur, inventor, physicist, researcher, scientist

🔊 26 Verb and noun collocations: science
come up with a solution, create an invention, design a device, develop a product, discover something, do an experiment, invent a product, investigate something, make a discovery, research something

🔊 27 Describing products
comfortable/uncomfortable, easy to use/hard to use, expensive/inexpensive/cheap, handy, high quality/low quality, innovative, practical/impractical, reliable/unreliable, useful/useless, well made/badly made, wearable, wireless

57

4 Project

WDYT? (What do you think?)

What makes a good invention? What's the best way to present it to people?

TASK: You successfully applied to appear on a television show for young entrepreneurs.

Prepare a one-minute product pitch to ask for funding for a product you have invented.

Learning outcomes
1 I can present an invention as a product pitch.
2 I can use communication to persuade people.
3 I can use appropriate language from the unit.

Graphic organiser → Project planner p119

STEP 1: THINK

2 Read the Model project and discuss the questions in pairs.
  1 When do entrepreneurs have to give pitches?
  2 Who might listen to a pitch?
  3 What information should be in a pitch?

STEP 2: PLAN

3 Look at the products. Choose an invention, think of your own, or research one. Make notes for a pitch.
  - What is your invention/product called?
  - What does it do?
  - What are its selling points? Why/How is it unique?
  - Who is it for? Why would they buy it?
  - How much does it cost to make? What would you sell it for?

STEP 3: CREATE

4 Work in pairs. Read the tips in the Super skills box and practise saying the Key phrases with a partner.

COMMUNICATION

Using language to persuade people

Tips
Give people useful and relevant information.
Give convincing arguments to persuade them.

Key phrases
This amazing product is affordable and high quality.
This exciting product will be practical and well-made.
People will find it very useful / easy to use because …

5 Read the *How to …* tips on p119. Then use your notes from exercise 3 to write your pitch.

1 🎥 Watch a video of a pitch. Answer the questions.
  1 How did Oliver and Amelia come up with the idea for the product?
  2 Do they look and sound confident?
  3 Which information do they not include?
   - A description of the product
   - Who would find it useful
   - How much it costs to make the product
   - Where they would make it
   - How much money they need

Grammar and Vocabulary → Quick review p57

Model project

Sleep suit
Notes for product pitch

- Head torch
- Pocket for phone/music player

- Keeps you warm
- You can sleep in it and walk around in it
- It has a light and pockets
- Useful when camping, travelling, or staying at a friend's house
- Suitable for all ages
- Practical, comfortable and easy to use

STEP 4: PRESENT

6 Practise and revise your product pitch as necessary.

7 Present your product pitch to the class.

8 **Peer review** Answer any questions about your product.

Product Ideas

Need to get somewhere in a hurry? Our jet suit with five mini-jet engines lets you fly through the sky at up to 80 kilometres an hour!

The table tennis door is the ultimate solution for small spaces.

4 FINAL REFLECTION

1 The task
How successful was your product pitch?
How easy was it to produce it?

2 Super skills
How well did your group communicate?
How well did you use language to persuade?

3 Language
What new language did you use from this unit?

Beyond the task
Is it useful to be able to give a good presentation like this? Why?

When (else) do you have to give presentations? How do they differ from this one?

5 Smile!

WDYT? (What do you think?)

Who took the first selfie?

Vocabulary: describing art and photography; types of art and word families

Grammar: the passive: present and past; active and passive; the passive: questions and answers

Reading: an online article on wildlife photography

Listening: an audio guide at a museum

Speaking: talking about photos

Writing: an online post

Project: a timeline about the history of selfies

Video skills p61

Real-world speaking p67

Project pp70–71

Describing art and photography

1 Look at pictures A–E. Which one do you like best, and why?

2 ♻ Check the meaning of the words for describing art in the box. Which would you use to describe pictures A–E?

| abstract   boring   brilliant   colourful   funny |
| original   realistic   shocking   traditional   ugly |

3 Complete the diagram with the adjectives from exercise 2.

Positive opinions   **Negative opinions**
brilliant   *traditional*   *ugly*

4 🔊 28 Listen to two friends, Dan and Emma, discussing a work of art. Answer the questions.
  1 Which picture are they talking about?
  2 Who likes the work of art and why?
  3 Who doesn't like it and why?

60

Vocabulary 5

6 Copy and complete the table with the words from exercise 5.

nouns for photographic equipment	selfie-stick
other nouns	self-portrait
verbs for editing photos	add filters
other verbs	press the shutter
adjectives	close-up

7 💬 Work in pairs. Imagine you're teaching someone how to create the perfect selfie. Write a list of instructions.

How to make the perfect selfie.
1 *use a selfie-stick*
2 (…)

8 💬 Swap your instructions with another pair. Have they forgotten anything?

VIDEO SKILLS

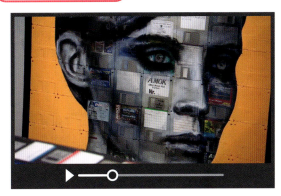

9 🎥 Watch the video and answer the questions.
1 Why is the video called 'A different kind of portrait'?
2 Would you buy this art? Why/Why not?

10 💬 Work in pairs. Discuss the questions.
1 What type of video is this?
2 Which adjectives describe the video: informative, entertaining, funny, dramatic, persuasive?
3 This video has voiceover over images of the art and footage of the artist working. Does this work well for this type of video? Why/Why not?

5  Complete the information about selfies with words in the box. Which fact do you think is not true? Listen and check.

> add filters   close-up   edit   go viral
> in/out of focus   lens   photogenic   photo shoot
> press the shutter   retouch   self-portrait   selfie
> selfie-stick   share   tripod

Selfies: amazing but true?

- The astronaut Buzz Aldrin took the first space **1** (…) in 1966.
- Makati City in the Philippines is the 'selfie capital of the world'.
- The first ever **2** (…) was painted by the 21-year-old Italian artist Parmigianino in 1524.
- The average age of selfie takers is 23.6, and is getting younger.
- Thirty-six per cent of young people admit that they retouch or **3** (…) to their selfies before they **4** (…) them online.
- Men take more selfies than women.
- You aren't allowed to use a **5** (…) at Disney parks or the Colosseum in Rome.

5 Reading and critical thinking

An online article

1 Describe the main photo on p63. Do you think it is a selfie or a portrait? Why?

▶ **Subskill: Using images and captions to help understand a text**

Images and captions can often give you clues about the key themes in an article.

2 Look at all the pictures on p63 and read the captions. Guess the answers for 1–3.
  1 Naruto is **a monkey/a wildlife charity**.
  2 David Slater **works for an animal charity/is a wildlife photographer**.
  3 David Slater gets **75%/25%** of the money from the photo.

3 🔊 30 Read and listen to the article. Check your answers to exercises 1 and 2. Which sentences in the text confirm the answers?

4 Read the information about macaques. Then match 1–5 with a–e to make sentences.
  1 Crested macaques are
  2 The macaque population has
  3 People who hunt macaques aren't
  4 The macaques' habitat is
  5 People sometimes

  a threatened by human activity.
  b called 'yaki' in Indonesia.
  c capture baby macaques.
  d been reduced by 90%.
  e often punished.

5 **Word work** Complete sentences 1–5 with the verbs in the box. Then find the expressions in the text and check the meaning.

| earn | own | raise | reach | sue |

  1 If you (…) the copyright of an image, you can decide how it is used.
  2 If you (…) someone, you make a legal complaint against them.
  3 You (…) someone's trust when you have a good relationship for a long time.
  4 Two people (…) a settlement when they agree on the result of a negotiation.
  5 Wildlife charities often (…) awareness of endangered species.

6 Read the text again and answer the questions.
  1 Why couldn't David Slater make money from the photo?
  2 What is PETA?
  3 Why did PETA say that Naruto owned the copyright?
  4 Where did David take the photos of the macaques?
  5 What did David do to make the monkey selfie possible?
  6 Who won the legal battle?

7 Choose the best option to complete the sentences, according to the text.
  1 David Slater (…)
    a sued Naruto
    b was a member of PETA
    c wanted to help the endangered monkeys
  2 Naruto (…)
    a helped David to set up the photographic equipment
    b used David's camera to take a selfie
    c was captured by a hunter
  3 In the settlement, David Slater agreed (…)
    a to adopt Naruto
    b not to use the monkey selfie
    c to give money to charity every time the monkey selfie is used

8 💬 Work in pairs. In your opinion, why does David Slater say 'Every photographer dreams of a photograph like this'? Discuss.
  • fame
  • personal satisfaction
  • money
  • professional success

CRITICAL THINKING *SUPER SKILLS*

  1 **Apply** Who owns your photos? Identify all the places where your photos are published. Write a list. Think about:
    a photos that you take and share
    b photos of you that other people take
  2 **Analyse** Who do you think should own copyright of the photos in a and b above? Is it the person who takes the photo, the person who appears in the photo, or the place where the photo is published?
  3 **Evaluate** Identify situations where this could be a problem.

Research

Find out who owns the copyright in photos that are shared online.

SMILE PLEASE!

It's monkey business for wildlife photographer

'Every photographer dreams of a photograph like this,' says British wildlife photographer David Slater, speaking to *The Guardian* newspaper. You have to admit it's an amazing picture – a close-up portrait of a macaque with his fabulous smile. The picture soon went viral on social media, but Slater couldn't make money from it because people argued that he didn't own the copyright. A macaque called Naruto had taken the photo. It was the first ever monkey selfie!

But can a monkey **own** copyright? This was the subject of a two-year legal battle. After the photos were published in a book called *Wildlife Personalities*, Slater was **sued** by Naruto. The monkey was represented by PETA (People for the Ethical Treatment of Animals), who argued that Naruto owned the copyright, since he had taken the photo. Slater argued that he was the owner of this image and all the others that he took while he was working with the macaques on the Indonesian island of Sulawesi.

It's true that one of the monkeys pressed the shutter for this photo, but only after Slater had already spent days **earning** their trust while he was setting up the photo shoot in the tropical forest. The tripod wasn't set up by Naruto, he argued. The lighting and the composition and the background weren't designed by the monkey.

Eventually a settlement was **reached**. Judges agreed that Slater was the legal owner of the monkey selfie, and Slater agreed to donate 25% of the money from it to wildlife charities that protect the macaques. Although he hopes never to fight another legal battle with a macaque, Slater is glad that his photos have **raised** awareness. 'Hopefully the picture contributed to saving the species,' he says to *The Guardian*. 'That was the original intention all along.'

Wildlife charities now benefit every time Naruto's photo is used.

The crested macaques, known locally as 'yaki', are an endangered species in Indonesia. Their population has decreased by 90% in the last 30 years – there are now only a few thousand left in the wild. Although it's illegal to hunt macaques, the hunters aren't usually arrested, and baby monkeys are often adopted as family pets. The animals are also forced out of their habitat by human activity.

Photographer David Slater was sued by a macaque from Indonesia.

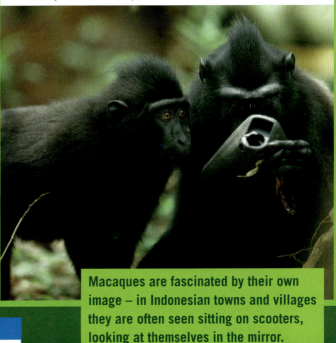

Macaques are fascinated by their own image – in Indonesian towns and villages they are often seen sitting on scooters, looking at themselves in the mirror.

Did you know?

Copyright is the legal right to have control over your creative work. If you own the copyright in something, other people must pay you if they want to use it.

5 Grammar

The passive: present and past

1 Read the examples and choose the correct options according to the article on p63. Then answer questions 1–2.

Present simple passive
The photos of Naruto **are**/**aren't** shared a lot online. Wildlife charities receive money when Naruto's selfie **is**/**isn't** used.
Past simple passive
David's wildlife photos **were**/**weren't** published. The photographer **was**/**wasn't** sued.

1 Which auxiliary verb do we use to form the passive?
  a have   b be
2 In passive sentences, who/what is more important?
  a the person/object that experiences the action
  b the person/object that performs the action

2 Complete the information with the correct present simple passive form of the verbs.

 How to … take WILDLIFE photos

- It's important not to disturb wildlife. The best photos 1 (…) (**take**) from a distance.
- Think about what wildlife 2 (…) (**find**) in your local area. You can practise on flowers and insects.
- Smartphones 3 (…) (**not design**) for wildlife photography but you can buy special telephoto lens attachments.
- Make sure the flash 4 (…) (**turn off**).
- Don't give up – hours can pass before the perfect animal 5 (…) (**see**).

3 Complete the sentences with the correct past passive form of the verbs in brackets.

1 The first Wildlife Photographer of the Year competition *was held* (**hold**) in 1964.
2 I entered two photos last year but unfortunately they (…) (**not select**).
3 I (…) (**not give**) a prize last year but hopefully I'll be luckier next year!
4 All the winning photos (…) (**exhibit**) at the Natural History Museum in London.
5 About 50,000 photos (…) (**send**) from 92 countries around the world.
6 My favourite was a photo of a fox, which (…) (**take**) by Ashleigh Scully.

Active and passive

4 Read the examples. Then choose the correct words.

Active	The monkey took the selfie.
Passive	The selfie was taken by the monkey.

1 In the active sentence, the blue words are the **subject**/**object**.
2 In the passive sentence, the blue words are the **subject**/**object**.
3 In passive sentences, we use **by**/**for** to say who performs an action.

5 Rewrite the sentences using the present or past passive. In which sentences is *by* not necessary?

1 Naruto pressed the shutter. The shutter (…) .
2 Naruto didn't set up the tripod. The tripod (…) .
3 People sometimes hunt baby macaques. Baby macaques (…) .
4 People in Indonesia call the macaques 'yaki'. The macaques (…) .

6 Read the text and choose the correct passive or active verbs.

Fourteen-year-old Laura Albiac **1 chose/was chosen** as a finalist in the Wildlife Photographer of the Year competition for her photo of an Iberian lynx. The photo **2 took/was taken** in the Sierra de Andújar National Park. Today the Iberian lynx **3 finds/is found** only in southern Spain – it's an endangered species that **4 protects/is protected** by law.

Laura, who lives near Barcelona, **5 travelled/was travelled** to the park in Jaén province with her family. They **6 waited/were waited** for two days before their patience **7 rewarded/was rewarded**: there were two wild lynx just metres from the road. Laura **8 watched/was watched** for more than an hour.

7 Answer the question to solve the Brain teaser.

These creatures sleep in trees, in nests which are made of leaves. In the wild, they're found only in Africa. They're very intelligent – one of these creatures was sent into space in 1961!

Can you guess the animal?

Pronunciation: weak forms: /ə/ with was /wəz/ and were /wə/ → p117

Vocabulary and Listening 5

Types of art

1 🔊 31 Listen and repeat the words. Which types of art do you like?

- graffiti art
- pottery
- sculpture
- installation art
- painting
- graphic design
- drawing
- printmaking
- photography
- fashion design

2 Read the information in the box. Then copy and complete the table.

> **Word families**
> Word families are groups of words with a common root. You can add suffixes or prefixes to make new words. For example, we often add *-er* or *-or* to a verb to make the noun for a person who does something.

verb	noun (artist)	noun (type of art)
paint	painter	1 (…)
2 (…)	sculptor	sculpture
3 (…)	designer	design
throw a pot	potter	4 (…)
take a photo	5 (…)	photography
make a 6 (…)	printmaker	printmaking

3 💬 Work in pairs. Have you ever seen examples of the types of art in exercise 1?

> Have you ever seen any graffiti art?

> Yes, I've seen graffiti art at the skate-park near my house.

4 Match pictures A–E with questions 1–5 in the Art Quiz. Can you guess the answers?

Art Quiz

1. This Renaissance artist was born in Italy in 1452. His most famous painting is called 'Mona Lisa'.
2. This artist painted a lot of colourful self-portraits. She was born in Mexico in 1907.
3. This surrealist artist was born in Spain in 1904. He made paintings, sculptures, films and drawings.
4. This artist is famous for her installations and fashion designs. She was born in Japan in 1929.
5. This 'Pop Art' artist was a printmaker, photographer and film-maker. He lived in New York.

An audio guide

5 🔊 32 Listen to the audio guide about three art works. Which artists were they made by?

▶ **Subskill: Checking what information you need**
Before transferring answers into a table, make sure you know exactly what information you need to listen for such as names or dates.

6 Copy the table in your notebook. Then listen again and transfer the correct information into the table.

Work of art	1	2	3
Who was it made by?			
What is it called?			
When was it made?			

> **Research**
> Find images or videos of the three artworks. Which one is your favourite?

B Frida Kahlo
C Salvador Dalí
A Andy Warhol
D Yayoi Kusama
E Leonardo da Vinci

5 Grammar

The passive: questions and answers

1 Match example questions 1–4 with a–d. How are the passive short answers formed?

Present passive
1 **Is** Frida Kahlo's painting **exhibited** in Mexico City?
2 **Are** Yayoi Kusama's sculptures **made** of wood?
Past passive
3 **Was** Andy Warhol **born** in the USA?
4 **Were** Warhol's prints **created** in the 1960s?

a Yes, he was.
b Yes, it is.
c Yes, they were.
d No, they aren't.

2 Complete the questions with the correct form of the passive. Do you know the answers?
1 Leonardo da Vinci / be born / in Italy / ? (past)
2 da Vinci's paintings / make / in the 20th century / ? (past)
3 The *Mona Lisa* / exhibit / in Paris / ? (present)
4 da Vinci's art works / make / of plastic / ? (present)

3 Write the words in order to make passive questions.

Using the passive in *Wh-* / *How* questions
Where is the painting **exhibited**?
Who was it **made** by?
When was it **painted**?

1 installation / What / called / is / the ?
2 designed / was / Who / by / it ?
3 are / What / made / the figures / of ?
4 the figures / by / made / were / Who ?
5 in Liverpool / exhibited / the installation / Was ?
6 made / versions / many / How / were ?

4 Read about 'Field for the British Isles'. Then answer the questions in exercise 3.

Field for the British Isles

This installation, *Field for the British Isles*, was designed by the British sculptor Antony Gormley, but all the figures were made by schoolchildren with their parents and grandparents. About 100 students and their families made 40,000 clay figures in a week. The installation was exhibited at the Tate Gallery in Liverpool.

Five other versions of *Field* were also made: in Australia, Mexico, Brazil, Sweden and China. *Asian Field* had more than 190,000 clay figures!

5 Complete the questions using the correct past passive form of the verbs.
1 Who … it … (create) by?
2 What … it … (make) of?
3 Where … it … (exhibit) ?
4 In your opinion, why … it … (make) ?

6 Work in pairs. Follow the instructions.
Student A: Choose an artwork from Unit 5.
Student B: Ask questions to guess the artwork.

> Where was it made?

> It was painted in …

7 Complete the text with the correct form of the verbs in brackets.

GRAMMAR ROUND-UP
1 2 3 4 5 **6 7 8**

FaceApp: from grumpy to smiley!

Have you ever *visited* **(visit)** a museum and wondered why everyone looks miserable? British designer Olly Gibbs and his friend Bronwyn **1** (…) **(find)** a funny solution to this problem while they **2** (…) **(visit)** the Rijksmuseum in Amsterdam. They **3** (…) **(use)** FaceApp to put a smile on the face of all the old portraits – soon they **4** (…) **(transform)** . It's easy **5** (…) **(find)** grumpy faces in old-fashioned art – people rarely smiled because they **6** (…) **(not have)** good teeth!

The Rijksmuseum photos **7** (…) **(go)** viral since Olly **8** (…) **(share)** them on Twitter. Fortunately, the museum took it all with a smile!

Real-world speaking

Talking about photos

1 🎥 Watch a video of Emily and Malik talking about photos. Answer the questions.
1 Where did Emily go on holiday?
2 Who was the sculpture made by?

2 Complete 1–3 in the dialogue with these verbs in the box. Watch again and check.

   add   look   scroll

Malik
Hey, I saw the vacation photos you posted – they were great!

Emily
Thanks! Do you want to look at the rest?

Malik
Sure – I'd love to!

Emily
Here – you can just **1** (…) through them.

Malik
This one's amazing! Where was it taken?

Emily
Oh, that one was taken at National Harbor in Maryland.

Malik
It looks beautiful. Did you **2** (…) filters?

Emily
No, they haven't been edited. Honestly, it really looked like that!

Malik
And what about this one? What's that big sculpture in the background?

Emily
That's *The Awakening*, a very big sculpture. It was made by J. Seward Johnson.

Malik
Wow! Hey – I like this selfie, you **3** (…) great. But you look a bit sad.

Emily
Yes – that one was taken on the last day. It was the end of the vacation!

3 Read the Key phrases. Which phrases are said by the photographer?

4 Create your own dialogue. Follow the steps in the Skills boost.

SKILLS BOOST

THINK
Make notes about three photos from a holiday or trip, or from a magazine. Include:
- a landscape or view
- an object, building or work of art
- a selfie or portrait

PREPARE
Prepare a dialogue. Remember to include some of the phrases for talking about photos.

PRACTISE
Practise your dialogue. Use appropriate intonation for the exclamations.

PERFORM
Act out your dialogue for the class.

5 **Peer review** Listen to your classmates. Answer the questions.
1 Where were their photos taken?
2 Which of the Key phrases did they use?
3 Whose photo(s) do you like best?

Key phrases

I saw your (vacation) photos on Instagram.
Do you want to (have a) look at the rest?
This one's amazing/great!
Where was it taken?
That one was taken at/in …
It looks beautiful/so peaceful.
It looks like …/It looked like …
I like/love this one/this selfie!

 US ➔ UK

vacation (US) ➔ holiday (UK)

Phrasebook ➔ p124   67

5 Writing

arty-smarty.net

Photos | Art | News | Events   Subscribe

Old and new – have you spotted anything that reminds you of art from the past? *Send us your ideas!*

The Scream: original and modern

When I saw *The Scream: Bathroom Edition* by a Czech artist called Kristián Mensa on Instagram, I first thought of the emoji, but of course the original is by the Norwegian painter Edvard Munch.

Munch's original *The Scream* was painted in 1893. In the foreground there's a figure with a tortured expression – he seems to be screaming. In the background there's a red-orange sky and some dark blue water. There are also two figures in the background. Neither of them are screaming – they're just walking along a path.

The composition of Mensa's *Scream* is similar to Munch's painting, but it's a close-up of the face – the whole landscape isn't included. The face, hands and clothes are painted and there are three toilet rolls for the eyes and mouth.

These two works of art were made in different centuries but they have some things in common. Both Munch's figure and Mensa's figure have got a strange, shocking expression, and neither of them is smiling. I like both of them for different reasons – Munch's painting is more colourful, but Mensa's picture is funnier. Some people might think it's silly to make art with toilet rolls but I think it's brilliant!

Posted by Janek

The Scream

The Scream: Bathroom edition

An online post

1 Look at the two works of art in the online post. Do you know who they were made by? Read the text quickly to find out.

2 Read the text again and answer the questions.
   1 Where is Kristián Mensa from?
   2 When was Edvard Munch's *The Scream* painted?
   3 What can you see in the background?
   4 What is Mensa's work of art made of?
   5 What is the writer's opinion of the works of art?
   6 Which artwork do you like best? Why?

▶ **Subskill: Using *both* and *neither***

We use *both … and …* or *both of them* with affirmative verbs in the plural form.

Both Munch's figure and Mensa's figure have got a strange expression.

We use *neither … nor …* or *neither of them* with affirmative verbs. We can use the singular or plural form.

Neither of them is/are smiling.

3 Read the subskill information. Then read the online post again and find one more example of both and neither.

4 Read the text below and choose the correct words. Does the story have a happy ending?

Edvard Munch created several different versions of *The Scream* – two paintings, two pastel drawings and some prints. Both of the paintings **1 is/are** in Oslo, Norway – one at the National Gallery, and the other at the Munch Museum. Incredibly, **2 both/neither** of the paintings have been stolen – one in 1994, and the other in 2004. Fortunately, neither of the paintings **3 were/weren't** destroyed. Both of them **4 was/were** found later, and luckily **5 both/neither** of them were damaged.

5 Write an online post about two pieces of art. Follow the steps in the Skills boost.

Composition with Red Blue and Yellow by Piet Mondrian

The *Mondrian Collection* dresses by Yves St Laurent

SKILLS BOOST

THINK
Choose two works of art that have something in common. Use these images or your own ideas.

PREPARE
Make notes to describe and compare the works of art. Mention the subject/background/colours, and use *both* and *neither*.

Find out more information about the works of art, such as: *Who were they made by? When/Where were they made? What are they made of? Where are they exhibited?*

Make notes about your opinion of the works of art.

WRITE
Write your description. Use the online post on p68 and your notes to help you.

CHECK
Read your online post. Answer the questions.
1 Have you used present and past forms of passive and active verbs?
2 Have you included vocabulary about art and artists, and describing art?
3 Have you included examples of *both* and *neither*?
4 Have you written four paragraphs, including an introduction, the descriptions of two works of art, and your opinion?

6 Peer review Work in pairs. Follow the instructions.
1 Read your online post to another student, but don't say the names of the pieces of art. Can he/she guess from your description?
2 Listen to your classmate's description. Has he/she included all the things in the checklist?

QUICK REVIEW 5

Grammar

The passive (present and past): affirmative and negative
We use the passive when we don't know who does the action, or the action is more important than the person who does it.

Present simple passive
The photos of Naruto **are/aren't shared** a lot online.
Wildlife charities receive money when Naruto's selfie **is/isn't used**.

Past simple passive
David's wildlife photos **were/weren't published**.
The photographer **was/wasn't sued**.

Passive and active voice
Active The monkey **took** the selfie.

Passive The selfie **was taken by** the monkey.

The passive (present and past): questions and answers
Were the sculptures **made** by school children?
Yes, they were.
Is the painting **exhibited** in Mexico city?
Yes, it is.

Who **was** it **created** by?
What **is** it **made** of?
Where **is** the painting **exhibited**?

Vocabulary

🔊 33 **Describing art**
abstract, boring, brilliant, colourful, funny, original, realistic, shocking, traditional, ugly

🔊 34 **Photography**
nouns for photographic equipment: selfie-stick, lens, tripod
other nouns: self-portrait, selfie, photo shoot
verbs for editing photos: add filters, edit, retouch
other verbs: go viral, press the shutter, share
adjectives: close-up, in focus, out of focus, photogenic

🔊 35 **Types of art**
drawing, fashion design, graffiti art, graphic design, installation art, painting, pottery, sculpture, photography, printmaking

5 Project

WDYT? (What do you think?) Who took the first selfie?

TASK: Create a timeline about the history of selfies.

Learning outcomes
1 I can research the history of photography.
2 I can collaborate with others and be flexible to reach a common goal.
3 I can use the passive and active voice to give factual information about the past and present.

Graphic organiser → Project planner p120

1 🎥 Watch a video of students presenting their timeline about the history of the selfie. Look at their timeline in the Model project and complete 1–3 with the dates in the box.

| 2014 2003 1914 |

STEP 1: THINK

2 Write one sentence to summarise what happened for each date in exercise 1.
In 1914, …
In 2003, …
In 2014, …

STEP 2: PLAN

3 Work in pairs. Read the tip in the Super skills box and practise saying the Key phrases with a partner.

COLLABORATION

Being flexible to reach a common goal

Tip
When you work in a group, you can't always choose your favourite tasks!

Key phrases
Which topic would you like to research?
I'd like to research the one about …
My first/second choice would be …
I'm not so keen on …
I don't mind doing …
I'll do … if no one else wants to!

4 Work in groups of three. Research two of the topics each. Do you want to include any more topics? Use the tips and Key phrases in the Super skills box.
- Robert Cornelius' photographic self-portrait (1839)
- the first selfie in space (1966)
- Polaroid cameras (1970s)
- the invention of the iPhone (2007)
- the launch of Instagram (2010)
- *selfie* is 'word of the year' (2013)

STEP 3: CREATE

5 Work with your group. Share your research and put all the events in chronological order.

6 Read the *How to …* tips on p120. Then create your timeline.

STEP 4: PRESENT

7 Practise presenting your timeline. Record yourselves, and make improvements.

8 Present your timeline to the class. Answer your classmates' questions about it.

Model project

Timeline: the history of selfies

1839

This 'selfie in the mirror' was taken more than a century ago with a Kodak Brownie box camera. It was taken by 13-year-old Anastasia Nikolaevna, who was the youngest daughter of Russia's last tsar.

1 (…)

1966

1970s

The Sony Ericsson Z1010 was the first mobile phone with a front-facing camera, which was originally intended for video-conferencing. It had a 0.3 megapixel camera.

2 (…)

2007

2010

2013

3 (…)

A selfie-stick is a gadget which is used to take selfies from a distance. Although it was invented earlier, this was the year when selfie-sticks became popular around the world.

now

5 FINAL REFLECTION

1 **The task**
How successful was your timeline?
How easy was it to research and produce it?

2 **Super skills**
How well did you collaborate? Give examples.

3 **Language**
What new language did you use from this unit?

Beyond the task
Which things from the timeline can you remember happening during your lifetime? What do you think the future developments will be?

9 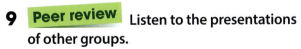 **Peer review** Listen to the presentations of other groups.
1 Which timeline is the most interesting?
2 Think of some questions to ask about the timeline.

6 Let's go!

WDYT?
(What do you think?)

How can travel help us to learn about the world?

Vocabulary: transport and travelling; extreme adjectives

Grammar: future tenses: review; present tenses with future meaning; future continuous

Reading: an interview about 'world-schooling'

Listening: a conversation about travel plans

Speaking: buying tickets / arranging travel

Writing: an opinion essay

Project: a map/itinerary for a world-schooling curriculum

Hot air balloons
Travel is all about getting **out of your comfort zone**, so how about taking a **trip** in a hot air balloon? You can **ride** above these beautiful rock formations in the region of 1 (…) .

Razzle Dazzle ferry
Sail across the River Mersey on this pop-art ferry. If you buy a **return ticket** and **set off** in the morning, you'll have time to visit the planetarium on the other side before you **come back** to 2 (…) in the afternoon.

Pedicab
While you're **on your travels** in 3 (…), take a **tour** of the top **tourist sights** in a pedicab. There are no **traffic jams** on Sunday mornings when the centre is closed to motor vehicles.

Video skills p73

Real-world speaking p79

Project: pp82–83

Transport and travelling

1 Look at pictures 1–5. Which types of transport can you see? Which one would be most fun, in your opinion?

> bus   cable car   camel   canoe   coach   ferry   hot air balloon
> moped   pedicab   plane   ship   train   tram   underground

2 Copy and complete the table with the words from exercise 1.

Travel by …	land (road/rail)	air or cable	water
	coach		

3 How do people get around where you live? Add more transport words to the table in exercise 2.

72

Vocabulary

Cable Car

If you aren't **afraid of heights**, you can **travel** all over the city of **4** (…) by cable car. It's the largest cable car system in the world, with 20 stations and six lines, like a 'metro' in the sky!

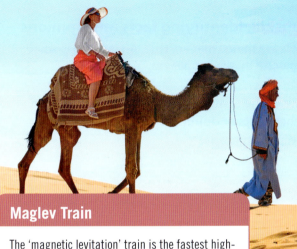

Maglev Train

The 'magnetic levitation' train is the fastest high-speed train in the world. If you need to **check in** at Pudong airport in **5** (…), the 30-km **journey** from the station will only take you seven minutes and 20 seconds, at a speed of 431 km/hour!

4 💬 **Work in pairs. Ask and answer about the types of transport in exercise 1. Who has used the most types of transport?**

> Have you ever travelled by ferry?
>> Yes, I have. I went by ferry to Staten Island when I visited New York.

Talking about how we travel
We travelled **by bus**. We didn't go **on foot**.

5 Read the mini-texts and complete 1–5 with five of the options in the box. Have you been to any of these places?

Mexico City, Mexico	Madrid, Spain
Liverpool, England	Washington D.C., USA
Cappadocia, Turkey	La Paz, Bolivia
Rome, Italy	Shanghai, China

6 🔊 36 **Listen and check your answers. Can you answer the Bonus Question?**

7 🎯 **Read the mini-texts again and check the meaning of the words in bold. Find:**

- three phrasal verbs
- three other nouns
- three other verbs
- three expressions
- three compound nouns

Confusable words
trip (n) journey (n) tour (n) travel (v)
travel (uncountable noun)

8 Complete the sentences to make them true for you.
1 My journey from home to school takes …
2 I usually set off for school at …
3 One of the best tourist sights in my region is …
4 From my town/city, it's easy to travel to …
5 I would be out of my comfort zone if I …

VIDEO SKILLS

9 🎥 **Watch the video and answer the questions.**
1 What places do you see?
2 Which place in the video would you most like to visit and why?

10 💬 **Work in pairs. Discuss the questions.**
1 What kind of video is this?
2 Why is this type of video popular?
3 When might people watch this type of video?

6 Reading and critical thinking

An interview

1 Skim the text quickly and choose the correct answers.
1 Miro is travelling because he's …
   a on a school trip.
   b a 'world-schooling' student.
2 Miro's experience of travelling has been …
   a more positive than negative.
   b more negative than positive.

2 🔊 37 Read and listen to the interview. Then write:
- two countries Miro has already visited
- four countries he'd like to visit
- four of his hobbies and interests
- his favourite subjects

3 Look at the interview and comments again. Correct one error in each sentence.
1 Miro started travelling last year.
2 At the moment, Miro and his mum live in a big city.
3 In the future, Miro wants to be an engineer.
4 JoGo and her family are travelling to America.
5 JoGo is setting off on Saturday.

4 Answer the questions with information from the text.
1 How many countries has Miro visited so far?
2 How does Miro define 'unschooling'?
3 According to Miro, what are the keys to successful travelling?
4 What is BlueSkyAnnie's opinion of world-schooling?
5 How is JoGo going to travel?

5 **Word work** In the interview, find the nouns that are used with adjectives 1–6. Then check the meaning of the phrases.
1 vibrant (…)
2 archaeological (…)
3 must-see (…)
4 like-minded (…)
5 spare (…)
6 favorite (US) (…)

6 Write:
1 an example of a region in your country that has got a vibrant culture
2 the name of an archaeological site in your country
3 two must-see places for visitors to your area
4 a place in your town where you can meet like-minded people
5 two things that you enjoy doing in your spare time
6 your three favourite subjects at school

▶ **Subskill: Identifying facts and opinions**
Facts are things that are true. An opinion is what someone thinks or believes.

7 Read the sentences from the interview. Are they facts or opinions? Do you agree with Miro's opinions?
1 'I've been to 14 countries.' _Fact_
2 'The world is full of places to explore.'
3 'It's foolish to stay in one place for the majority of your life.'
4 'There's a lack of community whilst travelling.'
5 'I can study what I want, when I want.'
6 'The world is a safe place.'

8 💬 Work in pairs. Answer the questions with your own opinions.
1 Would you like to have a world-schooling adventure? Why/Why not?
2 Where would you like to go?

CRITICAL THINKING
1 **Remember** Read the interview and comments, and find examples of the _advantages_ of world-schooling.
2 **Analyse** Are any _disadvantages_ mentioned in the text? Can you think of any more?
3 **Create** In your opinion, does world-schooling have more advantages or disadvantages?

Research
Find examples of other young people who have travelled the world instead of going to school.

Miro Siegel's real world-schooling adventure

A few years ago, Miro Siegel and his mother set off from their home in Los Angeles and began traveling. Since then, Miro hasn't been to school – he is being educated through 'world-schooling'. *Homeschooling Teen* magazine asked Miro about his experiences …

How many countries have you visited? Which one(s) did you like best?
I've been to 14 countries, and Guatemala and Peru are at the top. Guatemala for its colorful and vibrant culture, and Peru for its outstanding archaeological sites.

What other countries are on your list of must-see places you want to visit?
Greece, Turkey, Japan and India.

What do you like best about traveling?
Definitely the freedom that comes with it. The world is full of places to explore, and I think it's foolish to stay in one place for the majority of your life.

Is there a negative side to being a world traveler?
The largest problem I can see is that there's a severe lack of community whilst traveling. I have yet to meet any other like-minded people my age during my five years on the road.

What do you like doing in your spare time?
I read, write, or play video games. We're currently living in a mountain town and I enjoy hiking up the mountains.

How would you describe the concept of 'unschooling' and what it means to you?
Unschooling simply means I have the freedom to do what I want. I'm in charge of my own education, so I can study what I want, when I want and how I want.

Do you have any favorite subjects?
Literature is certainly at the top, and I like mythology.

What have you learned from your adventures?
I've learned that the world is a safe place, and that everything will work out in one way or another.

Where do you see yourself five years from now?
I honestly don't know. I haven't planned that far ahead yet. Eventually I want to become a writer, but I don't know how that's going to happen.

What would you recommend to other teens who might like to travel?
Don't be afraid, and pack light. Those are the two keys to travel. Be open to new experiences, and step outside of your comfort zone.

Comments

BlueSkyAnnie Sounds fantastic! Life's a journey – if you don't travel, you won't know what you're missing! Where are you going next on your travels?

JoGo My parents have decided to take me and my sister on a trip to Asia. We're going to Thailand and Vietnam and we aren't coming back until August. Our plane leaves on Monday – I can't wait!

US → UK

traveling (US) → travelling (UK)
colorful (US) → colourful (UK)
favorite (US) → favourite (UK)

6 Grammar

Future tenses: review

1 Read the examples and complete rules 1–3 with the words in the box.

> intentions   possibility   predictions

> Don't worry, everything will be fine!
> Jo is going to visit Asia.
> I might travel more when I'm older.

1 We use **will**/**won't** for future (…).
2 We use **be going to** for future (…).
3 We use **might**/**might not** for future (…).

> **Probably and definitely**
> The adverbs *probably* and *definitely* go after affirmative auxiliaries and before negative auxiliaries.
> I will probably travel when I finish university.
> I definitely won't leave school this year.

2 Complete the dialogue with *will / won't* or *might / might not* and the verbs in brackets.

A: Do you think Miro will become (become) a writer when he's older?
B: Perhaps! He **1** (…) (be) famous in the future.
A: I think he **2** (…) (definitely / have) some amazing experiences on his travels, but he **3** (…) (probably/not take) any formal exams.
B: So when do you think **4** (…) (you / leave) school?
A: I'm not sure yet. I **5** (…) (probably / leave) at 16 or 18. What about you?

3 Match sentences 1–4 with emoticons a–d. Then write them in order of probability.

 a   b   c   d

1 I'm probably not going to finish my project today.
2 I'll definitely finish my project today.
3 I definitely won't finish my project today.
4 I might finish my project today.

4 💬 Work in pairs. Imagine your classmate is going to leave school and go travelling. Write questions with *be going to*. Then ask and answer.

Where are you going to go first?
I'm going to go to Australia!

1 Where / go first?
2 Who / travel with?
3 Which subjects / study there?
4 How / prepare for the trip?

Present tenses with future meaning

5 Read the rules and examples. What are the negative and question forms?

> We use the present simple for future events that are part of a timetable or schedule.
> Our plane leaves at ten o'clock.
> We use the present continuous for future arrangements.
> We're coming back in August.

6 Complete the dialogue with the correct form of the present simple or present continuous.

A: Hi Ben, it's Adnan.
B: Hi Adnan, how are things?
A: Good, thanks. I'm calling about our trip to the Science Museum on Sunday.
B: Yes, great! What time *are we meeting* (we / meet)?
A: How about 12? The museum **1** (…) (open) at 11.
B: Yes, that's fine – I can meet earlier if you want. My brother **2** (…) (give) me a lift. **3** (…) (you / get) the train?
A: Yes – my train **4** (…) (not arrive) until 11:45, so let's meet at 12.
B: OK, no problem.
A: **5** (…) (your brother / come) to the museum with us?
B: No, I **6** (…) (meet) him later in town.
A: OK, cool. See you there!

7 Answer the question to solve the Brain teaser.

Travelling back in time?
Olga will be travelling on Flight XY3101 from New Zealand to Hawaii. The flight takes nine hours and 15 minutes, and the time difference between New Zealand and Hawaii is 23 hours. Olga's plane departs from Auckland airport at 00:15 and arrives in Hawaii at 10:30 the previous day and year!

What day of the year is Olga leaving New Zealand?

Pronunciation: *going to* /gənə/ → p117

Vocabulary and Listening 6

Extreme adjectives

> **Extreme adjectives**
> We use extreme adjectives to give emphasis.
> *interesting > fascinating!*

1 🔊 38 Match the extreme adjectives in A with the adjectives that have a similar meaning in B. Then listen and check.

A

| amazing ancient awful delicious delighted |
| exhausted freezing huge tiny unforgettable |

B

| bad big cold happy memorable |
| nice old tasty tired small |

2 🔊 39 Rewrite the text changing the normal adjectives to extreme adjectives. Then listen and check your answers.

> I've just heard about a young woman called Vedangi Kulkarni who's going to cycle round the world. What a **1 big** challenge! She'll be **2 tired** when she finishes but I'm sure she'll have a **3 nice** time. It'll be a **4 memorable** trip – she's going to travel through 15 countries across four continents. I bet she'll be **5 happy** if she succeeds!

> **Extreme adverbs of degree**
> With extreme adjectives, we don't use normal adverbs of degree.
> ~~quite~~ ✗   ~~very~~ ✗
> really ✓   absolutely ✓
> We had an **absolutely unforgettable** trip!

3 Answer the questions with extreme adverbs of degree and extreme adjectives. Do you know where these places are?
1. Are the paellas in Valencia tasty? **(delicious)**
   Yes, they are. They're really delicious!
2. Are the Giza pyramids old? **(ancient)**
3. Is Istanbul a big city? **(huge)**
4. Is it cold in winter in Siberia? **(freezing)**
5. Is Monaco a small country? **(tiny)**
6. Is the Yucatán Peninsula a nice place to visit? **(amazing)**

A conversation

4 🔊 40 Listen to Eva and Matthew's conversation about Vedangi Kulkarni. Answer the questions.
1. What do they think of Vedangi's travel plans?
2. Would they like to go on a similar trip?

5 Listen again and choose the correct options in the Fact file.

FACT FILE

Vedangi Kulkarni

Occupation: Studies **1** sports management/economics at Bournemouth University.
Age: 2 19/21 years old
Country of origin: 3 Britain/India
Current objective: To cycle around the world in **4** 80/100 days and **5** film/write about her journey.
Previous trips include: Cycling **6** from London to Brighton/across the Himalayas.

▶ **Subskill: Following a conversation**

We use certain words to introduce important points (e.g. *Basically, … / Apparently, … / So, …*) or examples (e.g. *For example, … / Like, …*).

6 Listen again and answer the questions. Listen carefully for the words in the Subskill.
1. Why does Vedangi want to complete her trip in 100 days?
2. What is the current world record?
3. How many kilometres will Vedangi have to cycle every day?
4. How far is the trip in total?
5. Where will Vedangi's journey begin and end?
6. How old was Vedangi when she went on her first big bike trip?

7 What do you think of Vedangi's plans? Write three sentences. Use extreme adverbs and adjectives in your answers.

Pronunciation: syllables and word stress with extreme adverbs and adjectives ➔ p117

77

6 Grammar

Future continuous

1 Look at the examples and answer the questions.

> Vedangi **will be finishing** her trip in about three months' time.
> I **won't be cycling around the world** when I'm 19!
> **Will she be cycling** alone?
> Yes, **she will**. / No, **she won't**.

1 What form is the verb after *will/won't + be*?
2 Do we use the verb in short answers?

2 Complete the sentences with the future continuous form of the verbs.
1 Vedangi (…) **(finish)** her trip in about three months' time.
2 I (…) **(not cycle)** round the world when I'm 19!
3 We (…) **(study)** when we're her age.
4 (…) **(you / go)** for a bike ride next weekend?
5 I (…) **(do)** my English homework on Saturday.

3 Look at the itinerary and complete the sentences. Use the future continuous.

> **Three Cities tour: itinerary**
> Monday — fly to Barcelona
> Tuesday — visit Barcelona
> Wednesday — travel to Paris
> Thursday — go on a boat trip
> Friday — take the train to London
> Saturday — go sight-seeing
> Sunday — return to the USA

1 *On Monday they'll be flying to Barcelona.*
2 On Tuesday (…)
3 On Wednesday (…)
4 On Thursday (…)
5 On Friday (…)
6 On Saturday (…)
7 On Sunday (…)

4 Complete the time expressions with the correct words.

> in   on   at   next   when

1 (…) this time tomorrow/11 o'clock tonight
2 (…) two weeks' time/September
3 (…) your birthday/Monday morning
4 (…) you've got time/you're older
5 (…) summer/weekend

5 Work in pairs. Choose the correct time expressions. Then ask and answer.

What will you be doing …
1 **after/next** this lesson?
2 **when/at** nine o'clock this evening?
3 **at/on** this time tomorrow?
4 **next/last** Saturday afternoon?
5 **at/in** August?
6 **this time/when** you're 22?

> What will you be doing after this lesson?

> I'll be taking a break before the maths lesson!

6 Choose the correct option.

GRAMMAR ROUND-UP
1 2 3 4 5 6 **7** 8

My Travel Diary

Day 5: Friday

We **1 've/'d** just arrived in London (on the train from Paris) and we're having coffee in St Pancras Station. There's a piano in the middle of the station and there's a girl **2 which/who** is playing some amazing music. Apparently the piano **3 gave/was given** to the station by Sir Elton John. Well, I'm so happy that I'm travelling! I **4 had never been/never went** to Europe before this trip but I definitely want to come back. Tomorrow morning we **5 visit/will be visiting** the Tate Modern art gallery. We **6 're going to take/take** the cable car across the River Thames! Unfortunately that **7 will be being/will be** our last day, because our flight **8 leaves/is leaving** really early on Sunday morning…

> **Research**
>
> Find out about the places in the travel diary.

Real-world speaking

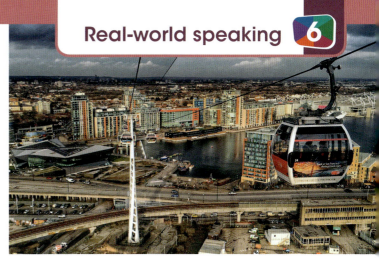

Buying tickets

1 🎥 Watch the video and complete 1–4 in the dialogue. How is Kate travelling?

Ticket agent: Can I help you?
Kate: Yes, I'd like tickets for the cable car, please.
Ticket agent: Are you travelling now?
Kate: Yes – how long does it take?
Ticket agent: About **1** (…) minutes. Single or return?
Kate: Two singles, please – we'll be coming back on the Tube.
Ticket agent: OK. Are you over 15?
Kate: Yes – we're both **2** (…). How much is it?
Ticket agent: It's **3** (…) single, so that'll be £9.00, please.
Kate: £9.00?
Ticket agent: Yes. Are you paying cash or card?
Kate: Er, I'll pay **4** (…) please.
Ticket agent: Thanks. You get on just over there.
Kate: Great, thanks!

2 Watch again and answer the questions.
1 Why doesn't Kate buy return tickets?
2 Why do you think the ticket agent asks Kate about her age?
3 What is the advantage of doing this journey by cable car, in your opinion?

3 Read the Key phrases. Who says each question, the ticket agent or the customer?

4 Create your own dialogue. Follow the steps in the Skills boost.

MERSEY *Ferries*
Single: £1.30 (child) / £2.70 (over 15)
Return: £1.70 (child) / £3.50 (over 15)
Ferries every 20 minutes.
Journey time 10 minutes.

SKILLS BOOST

THINK
Look at the information and think about your journey. Will you need a single or return? How many people are travelling? How are you going to pay?

PREPARE
Prepare your dialogue. Use the Key phrases and the model dialogue to help you.

PRACTISE
Practise your dialogue. Remember to use intonation to make your questions clear.

PERFORM
Act out your dialogue for the class.

5 **Peer review** Listen to your classmates. Answer the questions.
1 Do they ask the right questions?
2 Which Key phrases do they use?
3 Do they make their questions clear?

Key phrases
Can I help you? / Are you travelling now? / How long does it take? / Single or return? / How much is it? / Are you paying cash or card?

Real-world grammar
Er, I'**ll pay** cash please.

Phrasebook → p124

79

6 Writing

'International travel is the best way to learn about the world.'

Do you agree or disagree with this opinion?

1 Nowadays, it is becoming easier and cheaper to travel to distant places. In my opinion, international travel is the best way to learn about the world for several reasons.

2 First of all, I think that we can meet amazing people and explore different cultures when we travel. We can also practise speaking languages and learn new ones. In my view, this cultural exchange will help people to cooperate better and live in peace.

3 In addition, it seems to me that travelling forces us out of our comfort zone. Things might go wrong on our travels but we will learn to be more independent. Some people think that it's enough to read about the world or take a virtual tour of famous tourist sight, but I disagree. I don't think that these activities can replace real travel.

4 In conclusion, I believe that international travel is definitely the most inspiring way to learn about the world, and about ourselves. I'll soon be planning my next amazing adventure!

By Katy

An opinion essay

1 Read Katy's essay. Does she agree or disagree with the quotation?

2 Read the essay again. Which reasons does Katy give to support her opinion?
- meet amazing people
- explore different cultures
- learn new languages
- visit the main tourist sight
- step out of your comfort zone
- become more independent

3 Match paragraphs 1–4 in the essay with four items from a–e. Which one is <u>not</u> in the opinion essay?
- a the main reason why you agree/disagree
- b concluding paragraph
- c introduction to the essay
- d whole paragraph about a different opinion
- e additional reason why you agree/disagree and short reference to a different opinion

▶ Subskill: Giving opinions

I (don't) think/believe that …

In my view/opinion, …

It seems to me that …

As far as I can see, …

I'm not sure if/whether …

4 Read the subskill information. How many of the phrases for giving opinions can you find in Katy's essay?

5 Complete the sentences with phrases for giving opinions to make them true for you.
1 (…) it's better to explore your own region than travel abroad.
2 (…) the region where I live is a great place to visit.
3 (…) we can learn a lot by visiting new places.
4 (…) you can meet amazing people wherever you are.
5 (…) local travel is cheaper than international travel.

QUICK REVIEW 6

6 Write an opinion essay to answer the question. Follow the steps in the Skills boost.

'There's so much to learn from exploring my own region/country!' Do you agree or disagree?

SKILLS BOOST

THINK
1 Decide if you agree or disagree with the statement.
2 Write a list of reasons to support your opinion.

PREPARE
Organise your ideas into paragraphs. Use the model essay to help you.

Paragraph 1: introduction to the essay

Paragraph 2: the main reason why you agree/disagree

Paragraph 3: additional reason why you agree/disagree, and short reference to a different opinion

Paragraph 4: concluding paragraph

WRITE
Write your opinion essay. Remember to use phrases for giving opinions.

CHECK
Read your essay. Answer the questions.
1 Have you written four paragraphs?
2 Have you included phrases for opinions?
3 Have you used at least three examples of future tenses?
4 Have you used vocabulary about travelling and extreme adjectives?

7 **Peer review** Work in pairs. Exchange your essay with another student. Answer the questions.
1 Does your classmate agree or disagree with the question / with you?
2 How many reasons does your classmate give for his/her opinions?
3 Has he/she used grammar and vocabulary from this unit?

Grammar

Future tense review (*will/might/be going to*)
We use *will/won't* for future predictions.
*Don't worry, everything **will** be fine!*
We use *be going to* for future intentions.
*Jo **is going to** visit Asia.*
We use *might/might not* for future possibility.
*I **might** travel more when I'm older.*
The adverbs *probably* and *definitely* go after affirmative auxiliaries and before negative auxiliaries.
*I **will probably** travel when I finish university.*
*I **definitely won't** leave school this year.*

Present tenses for future meaning
We use the present simple for future events that are part of a timetable or schedule.
*Our plane **leaves** on Monday.*
We use the present continuous for future arrangements.
*We're **coming** back in August.*

Future continuous
We use the future continuous to talk about unfinished actions in the future. We only use the future continuous with action verbs (not stative verbs).
*On her world trip, Vedangi **will be cycling** through 15 different countries.*
*She **won't be riding** across the oceans!*
***Will** she **be cycling** every day?*
*Yes, **she will**. / No, **she won't**.*

Vocabulary

🔊 41 Transport
bus, cable car, camel, canoe, coach, ferry, hot air balloon, moped, pedicab, plane, ship, train, tram, underground

🔊 42 Travelling
journey, ride, sail, travel, trip, tour
tourist sight, traffic jam, return ticket
check in, come back, set off
(go/be) on your travels
(be) afraid of heights
(be/get) out of your comfort zone

🔊 43 Extreme adjectives
amazing, ancient, awful, delicious, delighted, exhausted, freezing, huge, tiny, unforgettable

6 Project

WDYT?
(What do you think?)

How can travel help us to learn about the world?

TASK: Create an itinerary for your ideal 'world-schooling' curriculum, and track it on a map.

Learning outcomes
1 I can plan, create and present an itinerary for a world-schooling curriculum.
2 I can use visuals to improve a creative project.
3 I can use appropriate language from the unit.

Graphic organiser → Project planner p120

1 Watch a video of students presenting their world-schooling itinerary. Answer the questions.
   1 Which four countries do they talk about?
   2 Which place are they going to visit in each country?

STEP 1: THINK

2 Look at plans A–D in the model itinerary on p83 and match them with school subjects in the box. There may be more than one possible answer.

| art   citizenship   foreign languages   geography |
| history   literature   maths   science |

STEP 2: PLAN

3 Work in pairs. Follow the instructions.
   1 Choose four school subjects from exercise 2.
   2 Divide the subjects between you and decide which places you're going to visit for each one.

4 Make notes about what you will do in each place on your itinerary. Use plans A–D in the Model project to help you.

STEP 3: CREATE

5 Work in pairs. Read the tips in the Super skills box and practise saying the Key phrases with a partner.

CREATIVITY — SUPER SKILLS

Using visuals

Tips

Visuals such as maps, photos and graphics can make a presentation easier to follow as well as more attractive.

Consider using digital visuals if possible.

Key phrases

How shall we make it look more colourful/ attractive/interesting?

Shall we include a map/some photos?

Let's use different colours/fonts/headers.

We could draw/cut and paste/cut out some images.

How about using an interactive map/ digital template?

6 Read the *How to …* tips on p120. Follow the steps to make your own world-schooling itinerary and map.

82 Grammar and Vocabulary → Quick review p81

Model project

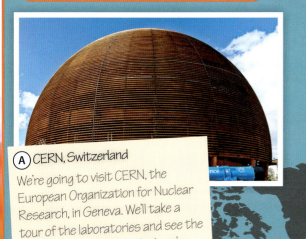

A CERN, Switzerland
We're going to visit CERN, the European Organization for Nuclear Research, in Geneva. We'll take a tour of the laboratories and see the Large Hadron Collider, which we've learnt about in our physics class. Hopefully we'll begin to understand the mysteries of the universe!

B Frida Kahlo Museum, Mexico
We're planning to go to the Frida Kahlo Museum in Coyoacán, Mexico City. We've studied her paintings in art class so it will be great to see them for real. We'll also see work by other famous 20th-century artists.

C Gallipoli Centre, Turkey
We learnt about the Battle of Gallipoli in our history class, so we're going to visit the Gallipoli Simulation Centre near Kabatepe. We'll also go to Anzac Cove and the war cemeteries.

D Shakespeare's Globe Theatre, UK
We're going to see Romeo and Juliet at Shakespeare's Globe in London – we've read the play in our English Literature class. We'll also take a tour of the theatre, and we'll learn more about Shakespeare's life.

STEP 4: PRESENT

7 Check the creative visuals in your project and practise presenting it.

8 Present your itinerary and map to the class. Explain where you're going to travel and why, and describe what you'll learn in each place.

9 **Peer review** Watch your classmates' presentations and vote for your favourite.

6 FINAL REFLECTION

1. **The task**
   How successful was your itinerary?
   How easy was it to produce it?

2. **Super skills**
   Did you use visuals creatively? Give examples.

3. **Language**
   What new language did you use from this unit?

Beyond the task
Is it possible to learn about the world without leaving your home town? Think about the places in your itinerary. Could you experience any of them without travelling? How?
We could take a virtual tour of CERN without travelling to Geneva.

7 Choices

WDYT?
(What do you think?)

Do we control technology or does it control us?

Vocabulary: IT; technology; phrasal verbs

Grammar: first, second and third conditionals

Reading: an infographic about digital DOs and DON'Ts

Listening: a radio phone-in about surviving without your phone

Speaking: giving advice

Writing: a report

Project: a questionnaire

Video skills p85

Real-world speaking p91

Project pp94–95

1 How many **apps** do you have on your phone?
   a Fewer than 50
   b More than 50

2 How often do you **check** your phone in a day?
   a 10–20 times
   b As often as I can!

3 How many **instant messages** do you **send** every day?
   a Only a few
   b Too many to count!

4 How often do you **update** your profile?
   a Never, I'm too busy.
   b All the time.

5 Do you always **tag** your friends in photos?
   a Tagging? What's that?
   b Of course!

6 Have you ever **posted** a comment or **uploaded** a photo and wished you hadn't?
   a Never
   b All the time!

7 Have you ever **deleted** a post?
   a Yes, I sometimes post things and then regret it.
   b No, I always think before I post.

8 Do you know how to **set** a safe password?
   a I don't use passwords on my devices – so boring.
   b Yes! Mine's 16 characters long.

9 Do you know how to **change** your privacy settings and **report** a problem?
   a No idea what that means!
   b Of course!

10 Have you **installed antivirus software**?
   a No, what's that?
   b Yes, and I check it regularly.

IT

1 Match images 1–8 with the words in the box. Can you add any more communication devices or parts of devices?

> app   comment   instant messaging   password   privacy settings
> profile   social networking sites   video game

2 🔊 44 Work in pairs. Listen to five descriptions and identify the things from exercise 1. Then describe the others for your partner to guess.

Vocabulary 7

What's your tech style?

Mostly A – You don't use technology much. It would be good to find out more about how it works!

Mostly B – You're pretty tech-savvy. You're careful how you use technology.

Did you know?
- The average person has 70–100 apps on their phone.
- The average millennial checks their phone 80–150 times a day!
- People upload 657 billion photos a year to social media sites.

Technology

3 Work in pairs. Check the meaning of the words in purple. Then do the quiz.

4 Use nouns in the box and verbs 1–8 to complete the collocations used in the quiz.

> a comment   a friend   a password   a photo
> a problem   privacy settings   your phone
> your profile

1 change (…)
2 update (…)
3 report (…)
4 post (…)
5 tag (…)
6 upload (…)
7 check (…)
8 set (…)

5 Look at the diagram and think about how often you do the things in exercise 4. Compare your answers in pairs.

NEVER   SOMETIMES   OFTEN   VERY OFTEN   ALWAYS

I never change my password. I sometimes …

6 Complete the sentences.
1 There aren't any cool a(…) for teenagers to use on their phones.
2 I don't know anyone who has r(…) an online problem.
3 It's important to c(…) your p(…) settings to protect your personal information.
4 You should regularly u(…) videos for your friends to watch.
5 You don't need to u(…) your p(…) . Nobody reads that information.
6 It's great when friends t(…) everyone in their photos.
7 I think most of my friends s(…) too many texts every day.
8 I know people who get anxious when they can't c(…) their phones – it's silly!

7 Discuss the statements in exercise 6 in pairs.

> Do you think there are any cool apps for teenagers? Which ones do you use?
>
> Yes, there are lots! I use (…)
>
> How often do you use them?

VIDEO SKILLS

8 Watch the video. What questions do the viewers ask the vlogger?

9 Work in pairs. Discuss the questions.
1 What is there in the video that helps you understand it? Think about text, the vlogger's voice, and the vlogger's body language.
2 Which vloggers are popular in your country and why?

Reading and critical thinking

An infographic

1 💬 Make a list of all the technology collocations you can remember. Compare them with your partner. Then scan the text – how many can you find?

2 🔊 45 Complete the statements with a number in the box. Then listen and check your guesses. Did any surprise you?

| 23 45 75 90 |

1 (…) % of young people tag their location in photos or posts.
2 (…) % of teenagers don't know how to change their privacy settings.
3 (…) % of teenagers have seen online bullying.
4 (…) % of teenagers have removed their names from photos they were tagged in.

▶ **Subskill: Understanding reference words**

Reference words are words like *it, his, she, these, this, that, them, herself, one,* etc. Understanding what they refer to helps you understand the meaning of the text.

3 Match the words in blue bold in the text to the people or things they refer to 1–6.
1 online bullying
2 teens
3 SamKing's friend
4 Cybergirl53
5 comments or videos
6 passwords

4 Can you find more reference words in the text. What do they refer to?

5 💬 Work in pairs. Read the statements and decide who or what the words in bold refer to. Guess whether the statements are true or false. Then read the infographic to check.
1 All teenagers know how to control who can see what **they** post online.
2 Less than 10% of teens have given **their** phone number online to someone they don't know.
3 Passwords should be private, you shouldn't share **them** with your friends.
4 More boys are bullied online than girls – **they** are twice as likely to be bullied.
5 When teens see bullying online, they always do something about **it**.

6 Read the text again and choose the correct answers.
1 After you have posted a video,
   a you can delete all copies of it.
   b you can make sure only friends can see it.
   c it is impossible to delete it everywhere.
2 What does the writer say about geotagging?
   a It means your family always know where you are.
   b You should know how to switch it off.
   c Only your friends will see the places you often go.
3 The writer advises people to
   a only talk to friends face-to-face.
   b not be rude when writing comments.
   c only share personal information with friends.
4 Which is false about passwords?
   a You should have a different one for each account.
   b An example of a secure password would be Mp55*H&m3.
   c Not many people used the passwords *superman* or *football*.
5 Online bullying
   a is something you should definitely report.
   b is less common than it used to be.
   c doesn't happen as often as people think it does.

7 **Word work** Match the words in purple bold in the text to the definitions. Write an example sentence for each word.
1 wanting to do or have something, especially something that is not good for you
2 very surprising
3 frightening or hurting someone who is weaker
4 feel sorry or sad that something has happened
5 feeling ashamed or shy
6 arrangements you have with email companies or Internet providers to use their services

8 💬 Work in pairs. Discuss the questions.
1 Which statistic surprised you most? Why?
2 What would you comment?

CRITICAL THINKING

Look at the infographic and follow the instructions.
1 **Understand** What information do the statistics give?
2 **Analyse** Why are these things problems?
3 **Create** Write a list of your top five tips for young people who are starting to use the Internet.

Digital DOs and Digital DON'Ts

23% OF TEENS DON'T KNOW HOW TO CHANGE THEIR PRIVACY SETTINGS

POSTING AND PRIVACY

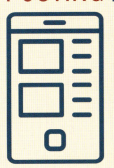

If you post something online, it will be available forever. Once you've written comments or uploaded videos, people can download them. You can delete something later, but you can't delete other people's downloads! It's not just what you post that matters – who sees it is just as important.

75% OF UNDER 24s GEOTAG THEIR PHOTOS ON SOCIAL MEDIA

TAGGING

Tagging your location (also called 'geotagging') in photos or posts seems like a fun way to tell your friends and family where you are – but potentially anyone could see your exact location or the places you often go. Find out how to switch geotagging off on your phone so you can control when to use it. Would you be happy if a friend tagged you without asking? Probably not! Forty-five per cent of teens say they have removed their name from photos that have tagged them, so check first.

DON'T GET PERSONAL

It's important to keep yourself safe so never give out personal information such as your address, your phone number, your date of birth or holiday dates.

THINK FIRST

Be polite when you write comments. It's easy to be rude online, but comments can really upset people. Only say things you would say to someone face-to-face.

PASSWORDS AND LOCK SCREENS

If your password is *123456* or *password*, you're using one of the top two worst passwords ever! Other popular 'bad' passwords include *superman* and *football*. If you don't use a secure password, your accounts won't be safe. Think of secure passwords for each account. These use a mix of lower case and capital letters, numbers and symbols. Also, use a pattern or PIN screen lock on all your devices. Having secure passwords or screen locks is no good if you share them – don't be tempted!

84% OF TEENS HAVE SEEN OTHERS TELL ONLINE BULLIES TO STOP

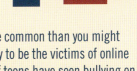

Bullying on social media is more common than you might think, and girls are twice as likely to be the victims of online bullying. An astonishing 90% of teens have seen bullying on social media. If you see it, or someone bullies you, report it.

1875 comments

 Cybergirl53 I've seen online bullying a few times, but I didn't do anything. I regret that. If someone bullied me, I'd tell my parents.

 SamKing Once, I tagged a friend in a photo and he was really embarrassed because everyone laughed at it. I always check now.

Did you know?
- There are 11 new internet users every second.
- This year, people will spend over a billion years online. (This is everyone in the world added up.)

7 Grammar

First and second conditional

1 Read the examples. Choose the correct answers to complete the rules.

First conditional
ACTION/SITUATION → RESULT
RESULT ← ACTION/SITUATION
If you post something online, it will be there forever.
My friends will see this photo if I upload it now.
What will you do if your phone breaks again?

1 We use the first conditional to talk about the result of a possible or likely situation in the **present/ future**.
2 We use *If* + subject + present simple, *will* (not) + **gerund/infinitive**.

2 Complete the sentences with the first conditional form of the verbs in brackets. Then add a comma where necessary.

Advice for Life!

1 If you (…) (reduce) your screen time you'll be happier.
2 You will learn more if you (…) (use) books rather than the Internet.
3 You (…) (not miss out) if you switch off your phone for a few hours.
4 If you (…) (not learn) how to use technology you won't get a good job.

3 💬 Work in pairs. Discuss the statements in exercise 2. Do you agree? Why/Why not?

4 Read the examples. Which part of the sentence expresses the action and which expresses the result?

Second conditional
I would be embarrassed if my parents saw my posts.
If I took a selfie that I didn't like, I wouldn't post it.
Would you be happy if a friend tagged you without asking?

1 We use the second conditional to talk about the results of imaginary situations in the present or future.
2 We use *If* + subject + past simple, *would* (not) + infinitive.

If I was or If I were
We sometimes use *If I were* instead of *If I was* in second conditional sentences.
If I were you, I wouldn't post that photo.

5 🔊 46 Choose the correct options. Then listen and check.

1 I'd text my friend if I **have/had** my phone with me.
2 What phone **would/did** you buy if you had lots of money?
3 I wouldn't play video games if I **wasn't/wouldn't be** bored.
4 Would you be happy if your parents **write/wrote** comments on your social network page?
5 If they weren't ill, they **were/would be** at school.
6 Would you buy an Xbox if you **have/had** the money?

6 Complete the first and second conditional sentences with the correct form of the verbs in brackets.

1 I'll phone Jack later if I (…) **(not see)** him on the way home.
2 If you don't let me use your laptop, I (…) **(not be)** able to email Maya.
3 I (…) **(not use)** that app if I didn't like it.
4 I won't charge my phone now if the battery (…) **(not be)** low.
5 I wouldn't buy a new phone if I (…) **(not need)** one.

7 Rewrite the sentences in exercise 6 with *unless*.

Unless
In first and second conditional sentences we can use *unless*. It means *if … not*.
I won't go to the party if you don't go.
I won't go to the party unless you go.
If I didn't like a photo, I wouldn't post it.
Unless I liked a photo, I wouldn't post it. / I wouldn't post a photo unless I liked it.

8 Answer the questions to solve the Brain teaser.

Dominic invited Azra and Carolina to his party.

Carolina: If I went to the party, I'd leave early.

Azra: If I go to the party, I'll leave early.

Who is more likely to go to the party?

88

Vocabulary and Listening 7

Phrasal verbs: screen–life balance

1 Complete the texts with the verbs in the box. Then answer the questions.

> chill get hang log meet
> print sign switch take work

1 Look at the photos – who isn't following their own advice?
2 Who do you think gives the best advice? Why?

If I want to 1 **chill** out, staring at a screen doesn't help. I go outside to relax. I try to get plenty of exercise. It's a good idea to 2 (…) up a sport like volleyball or an activity like dance. When you 3 (…) out, you improve your energy levels. It's fun too.
Lucy, 15

Chatting online is fun, but it's good to 4 (…) off after a while. It's important to 5 (…) up with friends in real life too! When you 6 (…) out with friends, don't spend all the time checking your phone. 7 (…) it off!
Sarita, 17

When I go on holiday, I like to 8 (…) away from all screens. I 9 (…) out of all social media sites until I go home! And when I'm working, I 10 (…) out documents to read. It gives my eyes a rest from the screen. I use recycled paper!
Mateo, 16

Separable and inseparable phrasal verbs

Inseparable verbs: the noun or pronoun must come after the preposition.
I *meet up with* my friends. ✓
I *meet up with* them. ✓   I *meet up* them *with*. ✗

Separable verbs: the noun can come before or after the preposition. The pronoun must come before the preposition.
Let's *take up* a new hobby. ✓
Let's *take* a new hobby *up*. ✓
Let's *take* it *up*. ✓   Let's *take up* it. ✗

2 Choose the correct answers.

1 When you finish on the computer, please (…).
   a log off   b log it off   c log off it
2 I started playing basketball last year. I'm so glad I (…).
   a took up   b took it up   c took up it
3 I see my friends at the weekend and (…).
   a hang out them with   b hang out with them
4 If you aren't listening to the radio, (…) it (…).
   a switch … off   b chill … out   c get … away

A radio phone-in

3 🔊 47 Listen to a radio phone-in. Which of the statements is true?

1 All the callers have given up using their phones.
2 All the callers are against teenagers using smartphones so often.
3 All the callers are talking about whether they could stop using their phones.

▶ **Subskill: Understanding sentence stress**
The stress falls on the important words and words the speaker wants to emphasise.

4 🔊 48 Read the extract from the radio phone-in and copy it into your notebook. Listen to the extract and underline the stressed words.

On today's programme we'll be talking about mobile phones … no, not the latest models or the best bargains. We'll be asking listeners an interesting question – could you survive without your mobile?

5 🔊 47 Match the people in the box and the decriptions. Then listen and check.

> The presenter Elif Pablo Basilio Sara Marek

1 doesn't think he/she would survive without his/her phone for a month.
2 sometimes uses his/her phone during the night.
3 would rather give up his/her phone than video games.
4 checks his/her phone as soon as he/she wakes up.
5 uses his/her phone to listen to music or play games.
6 once spent a month without using his/her phone.

6 💬 Work in pairs. Discuss the questions.

1 Which of your technology could you do without/not do without for a week?
2 Do you think it's a good idea to have technology-free time? Why/Why not?

7 Grammar

Third conditional

1 Look at the sentences and answer the questions.

A: I **played** games on my phone all the time and I **didn't pass** my exams.

B: If I **hadn't played** games all the time, I **would have passed** my exams.

1 Which sentence describes what actually happened in the past, A or B?
2 Which sentence imagines a different past, A or B?
3 Look at B. What do you notice about the affirmative/negative verb forms compared with A?

2 Read the examples and choose the correct options to complete the rules.

Third Conditional

ACTION/SITUATION → RESULT

If I'd got the message, I would have gone to the party.
I would have succeeded if you had done it with me.

1 We use the third conditional to talk about something in the past that did not happen. Since we cannot change the **future/past**, we can only imagine the situation and result.
2 We use If + subject + past perfect, would (not) have + **past participle/infinitive**.

3 Complete the sentences with the correct form of the verbs in brackets.

1 I didn't see Tom. If I (…) **(see)** him, I (…) **(invite)** him to the party.
2 They revised all weekend. They (…) **(not pass)** the exam if (…) **(not revise)** .
3 It was sunny yesterday. If (…) **(not be)** sunny, we (…) **(not go)** to the beach.
4 He didn't study. He (…) **(not fail)** the test if he (…) **(study)** .

4 Rewrite the sentences. Use the third conditional.

1 Jack went to bed late last night. He was tired today.
If Jack hadn't gone to bed late last night, he wouldn't have been tired today.

2 Kate was late for school. She didn't get up on time.
Kate (…) .
3 I dropped my phone. It broke.
If (…) .
4 I didn't do a digital detox. I felt stressed.
If (…) .

5 💬 Discuss in pairs. Use third conditional sentences in your answers.

What would you have done?

1 Your sister was in a supermarket and a person stole something. She saw it and told the manager.
2 A friend started a rumour about you. Everyone believed it.

6 Read the text and choose the correct option.

GRAMMAR ROUND-UP
1 2 3 4 5 6 7 8

If you didn't have anyone to sit with at school lunch, what **1** (…) you do? **2** (…) you ask to share a table with others and they say 'no', it's awful. High school student Natalie Hampton **3** (…) an app called *Sit With Us* to solve this problem. The app is free and students sign up to be 'ambassadors' at their school. Ambassadors post open lunches **4** (…) anyone can join. Students look on the app for an open lunch and they know they **5** (…) sit at that table. It's all private and there is no fear of rejection. Just one week after the app was released, over 10,000 people had **6** (…) downloaded it! Now, students **7** (…) it all over the world. If Natalie **8** (…) created this social media network, many more people would have been lonely at lunch.

1 a will   b did   c would
2 a Unless   b If   c Maybe
3 a creates b created   c was creating
4 a who   b where   c that
5 a must   b can   c will
6 a just   b yet   c already
7 a are using b used   c were used
8 a didn't   b hadn't   c wouldn't hace

Research

Find out about a project which uses technology to help others. Why do you think it's an interesting project?

Real-world speaking

Giving advice

1 Look at the photos. How do you think Emily feels?

2 🎥 Watch the video. Why does Emily need some advice?

Katya
Hey! You look upset. What's up?

Emily
Can I ask your advice? My friend Alex is 1 (…) at me and I don't know what to do.

Katya
What happened?

Emily
Well, I made a video of us skateboarding, and I put it online. When he found out, he was really angry.

Katya
Maybe you should have asked him first! How would you feel if someone did that to you?

Emily
A bit annoyed maybe, but I wouldn't really mind. I don't understand why he's so 2 (…).

Katya
Maybe he doesn't want videos of himself online.

Emily
You're right, I just forgot to ask. I thought he'd be 3 (…)! What would you do?

Katya
Well, you should apologize.

Emily
But he isn't answering my calls! What should I do?

Katya
If I were you, I'd go to his apartment. I think you should speak to him in person.

Emily
You're absolutely right …. But I'm really 4 (…).

Katya
You could write down what you want to say first and practice it. That might help.

Emily
Good idea, I'll do that. Thanks.

3 Watch again and then complete the dialogue with the words in the box.

| upset | mad | nervous | happy |

4 Watch again. Which Key phrase is not in the dialogue?

5 Create your own dialogue. Follow the steps in the Skills boost.

SKILLS BOOST

THINK
Read the task and make notes.
Your friend told you a secret and you promised not to tell anyone. You told someone else. Your friend is really upset.

PREPARE
Prepare a dialogue to talk to another friend about the problem. Remember to include phrases for asking for and giving advice.

PRACTISE
Practise your dialogue.

PERFORM
Act out your dialogue for the class.

6  Listen to your classmates and answer the questions.
1 Which situation did they choose?
2 Which Key phrases did they use?
3 Could they improve their dialogue? How?

Key phrases
Asking for advice:
Can I ask your advice?
What would you do (if …)? How would you feel (if …)?
What should I do? What would you do?

Giving advice:
If I were you, I'd …   You should/shouldn't have …
I think you should …   Why don't you …? You could …

 US → UK

annoyed (US) → cross (UK)
apologize (US) → apologise (UK)
apartment (US) → flat (UK)
practice (US) → practise (UK)

Phrasebook → p125   91

7 Writing

Screen and leisure habits in 15–18-year-olds

A This report outlines the results of a survey about screen and leisure habits. One hundred students aged 15–18 took part in the survey about how they use technology.

B Nearly everyone has access to a smartphone, only 5% do not. Almost half of teens go online almost constantly and just over a quarter go on several times a day. However, 12% go online only once a day. Only 8% do not go online every day. They use their phones to go on social media (92%), play video games (33%), listen to music (66%) and contact friends and family (100%). Around 55% of 16–18-year-olds say they would find it hard to give up social media if they had to, compared to 45% who say they wouldn't find it hard. Teenagers use their phones everywhere, the most typical places are at school, at home and while travelling. About 75% of teens have used their phones during the night and only 25% regularly switch phones off at night.

C In conclusion, almost all the teenagers use a smartphone regularly. The most popular things to do are use social media and contact friends and family. Over half the teenagers would find it hard to stop using social media. The results show that nowhere is technology free and night-time use is common.

A survey report

1 Read the report. Did anything surprise you?

2 Match paragraphs A–C with the descriptions 1–3.
1 gives some statistics from the survey results
2 has a summary of the results and conclusions
3 introduces the purpose and topic of the survey

3 Find equivalent numbers in the report. Then, write the expressions from smallest to biggest.
1 a third
2 a quarter
3 two thirds
4 less than 1 in 10
5 almost half
6 just over half
7 three quarters
8 more than 9 out of 10

4 Express each statistic in a different way.
1 48%
2 68%
3 one in five
4 78%
5 less than a quarter
6 over a third

▶ **Subskill: Using indefinite pronouns**

We use indefinite pronouns to refer to one or more unspecified people, places or things. Indefinite pronouns are always singular and have a singular verb, e.g. *Nothing is surprising when it comes to technology.*

5 Copy and complete the table with words from the report.

People	Places	Things
1 (…)/everybody	2 (…)	everything
someone/somebody	somewhere	something
anyone/anybody	anywhere	anything
no one/nobody	3 (…)	nothing

6 Choose the correct indefinite pronoun.
1 **Nobody/Anybody** wants to live without technology – everyone wants it!
2 I don't know **anything/anyone** who hasn't got a smartphone.
3 I need to buy **something/somewhere** for my brother. He loves gadgets!
4 If you could buy **anything/nothing**, would you buy a gadget?

QUICK REVIEW 7

5 Do you use your phone **somewhere/ everywhere** you go?
6 **Someone/Everyone** was looking at their screens. Nobody saw me.

7 Write a report. Follow the steps in the Skills boost.

> Look at the information. Write a report to describe the results of a survey on what teens do while watching TV.

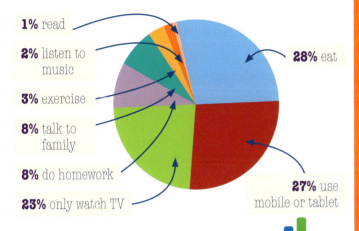

1% read
2% listen to music
3% exercise
8% talk to family
8% do homework
23% only watch TV
28% eat
27% use mobile or tablet

SKILLS BOOST

THINK
1 Look at the graphic and make sure you understand the information.

PREPARE
Make notes for the main points you want to include in the report. Decide how to introduce the report and your conclusions of the results.
Organise the information into three paragraphs. Use the model report to help you.

WRITE
Write your report.

CHECK
Read your report. Answer the questions.
1 Have you organised your report in three clear paragraphs?
2 Have you used indefinite pronouns?
3 Have you used a variety of ways to talk about statistics?
4 Have you included IT and technology vocabulary?

8 **Peer review** Exchange reports with another student and answer the questions.
1 Was the report clear and well organised?
2 Did they include useful vocabulary?

Grammar

First conditional
We use the first conditional to talk about the result of a possible or likely situation in the future.
If you **meet up** with friends, you**'ll have** fun.
If you **don't use** a secure password, your accounts **won't be** safe.

Second conditional
We use the second conditional to talk about the results of imaginary situations in the present or future.
If a friend **tagged** me, I **wouldn't be** happy.
I**'d tell** my parents **if** someone **bullied** me.

If/Unless
In first and second conditional sentences we can use *unless*. It means *if… not*.
I won't go to the party **unless** you go.
I won't go to the party **if** you do**n't** go.

Third conditional
We use the third conditional to talk about something in the past that did not happen.
If you **hadn't forgotten** your phone, you **would have been able** to text me.

Vocabulary

🔊 49 **IT**
apps, comment, instant messaging, password, privacy settings, profile, social networking sites, video game

🔊 50 **Technology**
change your privacy settings, check your phone, delete a post, install antivirus software, post a comment, report a problem, send (instant) messages, set a password, tag a friend, update your profile, upload a photo

🔊 51 **Phrasal verbs: screen–life balance**
chill out, get away from, hang out with, log off, meet up with, print out, switch off, sign out, take up, work out

7 Project

WDYT? (What do you think?)

Do we control technology or does it control us?

TASK: Write a questionnaire to find out about screen habits.

Learning outcomes
1 I can write a questionnaire and present it.
2 I can analyse and evaluate ideas to improve them.
3 I can use appropriate language from the unit.

Graphic organiser → Project planner p121

1 Watch the video of students presenting their questionnaire and answer the questions.
   1 How many questions did they ask?
   2 How many students completed the questionnaire?

STEP 1: THINK

2 Read the questionnaire and find an example of each question type 1–5.
   1 an open question where the answer could be anything
   2 a question with four options a–d to choose from
   3 a question where students rank answers on a scale
   4 a question with tick boxes where students can only tick one answer
   5 a question with tick boxes where students tick all answers relevant to them

STEP 2: PLAN

3 Work in groups. Read the tips in the Super skills box and practise saying the Key phrases with your group.

COLLABORATION

Working collaboratively to do a task

Tips
Make suggestions to your group and be open to feedback.
Listen to other people's suggestions and give feedback kindly. Be constructive.
Agree as a group on the best ideas.

Key phrases
What about …? / How about …?
That's a (really) great/brilliant/amazing idea.
(A chart) would be perfect/useful (for question 2).
I don't think that would work/help because …
I think it would be better to …
I agree / I don't agree (because …)

4 Work in groups. Decide your objective for the questionnaire. Choose one of the following subjects, or your own idea.
   • How much time do people spend away from technology?
   • Do people have good screen habits at bedtime?

5 In groups, make notes of the things you want to find out about.

STEP 3: CREATE

6 Read the *How to …* tips on p121 and write your questionnaire. Use the tips and Key phrases in the Super skills box.

7 Work in your groups. Follow the instructions.
   • Decide who will ask each question.
   • Ask as many classmates as you can.
   • Tell your group about your answers.
   • Work together to summarise the results. Add diagrams if you like.

Model project

Are you technology mad?

1 Which of these gadgets do you use every day?

☐ mobile phone ☐ tablet ☐ TV ☐ laptop/desktop computer
☐ video games ☐ digital camera ☐ CD or DVD player ☐ other

2 How many hours do you spend using technology/screens every day?

☐ 0–1 hour ☐ 2–3 hours ☐ 4–6 hours ☐ over 6 hours

3 How many apps have you got on your smartphone? Do you use them all?

4 If your house was on fire, would you …

   a pack a bag with all your gadgets before leaving – you need everything! ☐
   b definitely run in to rescue your smartphone ☐
   c leave but ask someone to rescue your favourite gadget ☐
   d get out and not worry about any gadgets ☐

5 Rank the statements from 0–5 (0 = I don't agree at all, 5 = I totally agree).

   1 When I'm waiting or I've got nothing to do, I need to use technology (e.g. my smartphone) to entertain myself. `0 1 2 3 4 5`
   2 If I'm out with friends, I don't use any technology at all. `0 1 2 3 4 5`
   3 I don't go anywhere without my smartphone. `0 1 2 3 4 5`
   4 Everyone can live happily without technology. `0 1 2 3 4 5`
   5 If I didn't have my gadgets, I probably wouldn't know what to do. `0 1 2 3 4 5`

STEP 4: PRESENT ●●●●

8 Present your questionnaire and the results to the class. Answer any questions about it.

9 **Peer review** Listen to the presentations of other pairs. What are the most surprising findings?

7 FINAL REFLECTION

1 **The task**
How well did you do the task?

2 **Super skills**
Did you analyse and evaluate ideas to improve them?

3 **Language**
What new language did you use from the unit? Give examples.

Beyond the task
In what situations might a questionnaire be useful? What are your tips for doing it well?

8 In the news

WDYT? (What do you think?)

How do we know if news is reliable?

Vocabulary: media and news; reporting verbs

Grammar: reported speech; reported offers, requests, suggestions and commands

Reading: an information leaflet about fake news

Listening: a radio news bulletin

Speaking: reacting to news

Writing: a news report

Project: report a news story

Video skills p97

Real-world speaking p103

Project pp106–107

World Cup winners announce wedding

source · broadcast · newsreader · mass media · BLOGGER · interviewee · TABLOID · pop-up ads · JOURNALISM · reliable · interviewer · trust · REPORTER · shocking · headlines

Media and news

1 Which types of media do you sometimes read/watch/listen to? In one minute, write a list of specific examples from your country.

Radio 1Xtra, Netflix, Kerrang!, …

2 ♻ Copy and complete the table with the types of media in the box. Which ones are more 'traditional'?

blog   magazine   podcast   newspaper   radio
satellite TV   social media   TV   website

Broadcast media:	*TV* (…) (…)
Print media:	(…) (…)
Digital media:	(…) (…) (…) (…)

Vocabulary 8

3 Look at the word cloud. Find words related to pictures 1–6.

1 journalism, mass media

4 Look at the word cloud again. Find the people to match definitions 1–5.
1 someone who interviews people
2 someone who is being interviewed
3 someone who reads the news on television or radio
4 someone who writes a blog
5 someone whose job is to write articles or make broadcasts about the news

5 Which words in the word cloud match definitions 1–6? Are they nouns, verbs or adjectives?
1 websites, newspapers, TV, radio, etc.
2 the activity of reporting the news for a website, newspaper, TV channel, radio programme, etc.
3 to feel confident that someone is honest and fair
4 someone/something that provides information for a journalist
5 someone/something that can be trusted to be accurate and truthful or true
6 extremely surprising or upsetting

6  Listen to four short extracts related to the news. Match them with a–d. Do you get the news from any of these sources?
a TV
b radio
c word of mouth
d podcast

7 Work in pairs. Discuss the questions.
1 What are the news headlines in your country today?
2 Where do you find out about the news?
3 Where do your parents find out about the news?
4 Which news sources do you trust most?

VIDEO SKILLS

8 Watch the video. Which headline do you think is true?
a Horse passes school exam
b Octopus predicts football result
c Reindeer forecasts the weather

9 Work in pairs. Discuss the questions.
1 How are text and images used in the video and why?
2 Which adjectives describe the video: informative, entertaining, funny, dramatic, persuasive?
3 Why are quiz shows popular?
4 What type of quiz shows are popular in your country?

8 Reading and critical thinking

An information leaflet

1 Read the definition of 'fake news'. Have you ever seen or read any fake news stories?

> **fake news**
> NOUN [UNCOUNTABLE] /ˌfeɪk ˈnjuːz/
> A story that is presented as being a genuine item of news but is in fact not true and is intended to deceive people
> *As a journalist I do not want to spread fake news.*

2 Look at the text on p99. What kind of text is it?
  a a news story about the health benefits of a new scientific product
  b advice for students about how to prepare for exams
  c an information leaflet that helps you to evaluate whether a news story is real or fake

3 🔊 53 Read and listen to the article. In your opinion, is the article a reliable source of information? Why/Why not?

▶ **Subskill: Navigating web pages**
  When you read a web page, look beyond the text. These things can help you to evaluate the reliability of the source: URL/web address, photos, adverts.

4 Look at the subskill information. What information in the text gives you clues about the reliability of the source?

5 **Word work** Find words or expressions in the text that mean:
  1 a special offer where you pay for two products and receive three
  2 pictures that have been changed digitally
  3 an interview with only one media company
  4 online adverts that open in a new window
  5 ask the same questions to a lot of people to obtain statistical information
  6 show the advantages of something

6 Complete the sentences with the correct words or phrases, according to the information leaflet.
  1 Reliable sources are more likely to have a tab where you can find (…) .
  2 The purpose of a headline is to (…) .
  3 The source could be unreliable if you can't find the name of the (…) .
  4 The images in fake news stories are often (…) .
  5 Most reliable news sites don't have (…) .

7 Read the leaflet again and answer the questions.
  1 Who is Noah Kidding?
  2 According to Kidding, what health conditions can be improved with his product?
  3 How much does a bottle of Fresh Mountain Air cost?
  4 What was the objective of Kidding's survey?
  5 Who is Wayne?
  6 How does Kidding obtain the bottled air?

8 Choose the best answers.
  1 Fresh Mountain Air (…)
    a cures many health problems.
    b contains more oxygen than normal air.
    c is the name of Noah Kidding's company.
  2 A reporter from News4You (…)
    a had bought two bottles of air.
    b interviewed Noah Kidding.
    c carried out a student survey.
  3 In the survey, (…) had consumed Fresh Mountain Air.
    a all the students
    b 50% of the students
    c only Kidding's family
  4 Fresh Mountain Air (…)
    a is only available online.
    b is sold by Noah Kidding.
    c is bottled at a factory.

9 💬 In pairs, answer the questions.
  1 Would you buy Fresh Mountain Air? Why/why not?
  2 Have you ever bought a product because you read about it or saw an advert?
  3 Do you think Noah Kidding is a genuine entrepreneur? Why/why not?

CRITICAL THINKING

1 **Understand** Look back at the text. How does it try to help people spot fake news? Why is it important for us to be able to spot fake news?

2 **Analyse** 'Fake news' was chosen as the 'word of the year' by a British dictionary publisher. What reasons can you think of for this? Think about world news over recent years.

3 **Evaluate** What could be the consequences of fake news? Can you think of any examples in your country or abroad?

How to spot fake news

If you see an interesting story online, can you trust it? Ask yourself these questions …

What's the source? Is this a reliable media organisation or the site of an individual blogger? Is there an 'About Us' section where you can find contact information?

What can the photos tell us? Fake news stories often use recycled or manipulated images. What is the source of the photo?

What's the whole story? Headlines are often shocking to attract the reader's attention. Can you find the same story on other websites or in print media?

Who's the journalist? Can you find the name of the reporter? If it's an interview, is the interviewee a real person?

Are there lots of ads? Fake news sites are often packed with annoying pop-up ads. Most reliable news sites limit their adverts.

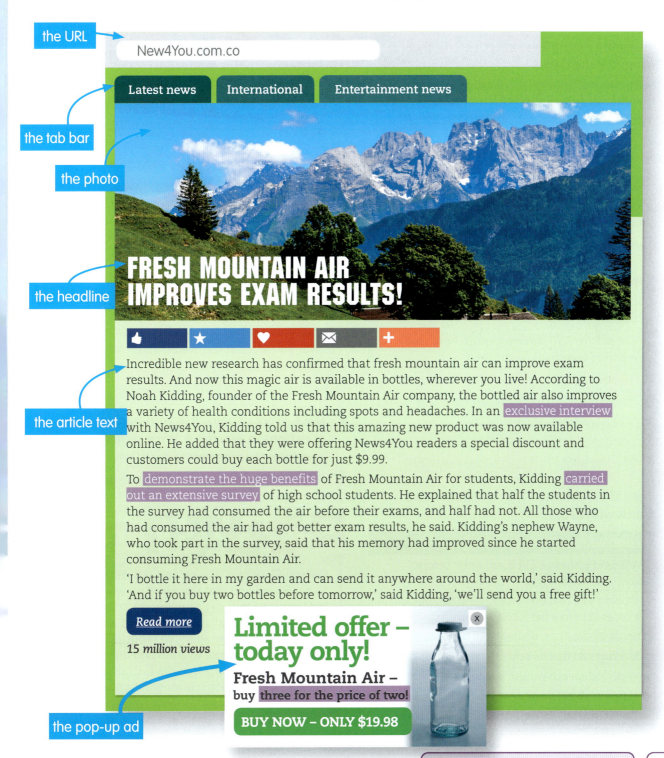

the URL — New4You.com.co

the tab bar — Latest news | International | Entertainment news

the photo

the headline — **FRESH MOUNTAIN AIR IMPROVES EXAM RESULTS!**

the article text — Incredible new research has confirmed that fresh mountain air can improve exam results. And now this magic air is available in bottles, wherever you live! According to Noah Kidding, founder of the Fresh Mountain Air company, the bottled air also improves a variety of health conditions including spots and headaches. In an exclusive interview with News4You, Kidding told us that this amazing new product was now available online. He added that they were offering News4You readers a special discount and customers could buy each bottle for just $9.99.

To demonstrate the huge benefits of Fresh Mountain Air for students, Kidding carried out an extensive survey of high school students. He explained that half the students in the survey had consumed the air before their exams, and half had not. All those who had consumed the air had got better exam results, he said. Kidding's nephew Wayne, who took part in the survey, said that his memory had improved since he started consuming Fresh Mountain Air.

'I bottle it here in my garden and can send it anywhere around the world,' said Kidding. 'And if you buy two bottles before tomorrow,' said Kidding, 'we'll send you a free gift!'

Read more — 15 million views

the pop-up ad — **Limited offer – today only!** Fresh Mountain Air – buy three for the price of two! **BUY NOW – ONLY $19.98**

8 Grammar

Reported speech

1 Read the examples. Can you remember who said what in the article on p99? Complete 1–4 with the people in the box.

> Noah Kidding   the reporter   Wayne

direct speech → reported speech
'Fresh mountain air *improves* exam results.' > The reporter said that fresh mountain air *improved* exam results. 'We're *offering* readers a special discount.' > Noah Kidding said that they *were offering* readers a special discount.

1 'Kidding *carried out* a survey.' (…) said that Kidding *had carried out* a survey.
2 'My memory *has improved*.' (…) said that his memory *had improved*.
3 'We'*ll send* a free gift.' (…) said that they *would send* a free gift.
4 'We *can* send it anywhere.' (…) said that they *could* send it anywhere.

2 Study the examples in exercise 1. Copy and complete the table.

Reported speech: tense changes	
Direct speech	**Reported speech**
present simple	(…)
present continuous	(…)
past simple	(…)
present perfect	(…)
future with *will*	(…)
can	(…)

3 Rewrite the sentences in reported speech.

1 'We're going to study reported speech,' said our teacher.
   Our teacher said that we were going to study reported speech.
2 'We love studying grammar,' said my classmates.
3 'I haven't studied reported speech before,' I said.
4 'It isn't easy,' said Nevin.
5 'I can't do this exercise,' said Pablo.
6 'The test will be on Monday,' said our teacher.

4 Read the examples. Then match the blue words with a–d.

Reported speech: other changes
'*We*'ll send *you* a free gift if you order before *tomorrow*,' said Kidding. > Kidding said that *they* would send *us* a free gift if we ordered before *the following day*. 'I bottle it *here* in *my* garden,' said Kidding. > Kidding said that *he* bottled it *there* in *his* garden. In reported speech we also change:
a subject/object pronouns   b time expressions c possessive adjectives   d adverbs of place

5 Look at exercise 4 again. Rewrite the sentences in direct speech.

1 Our teacher said that we had seen that article the week before. 'You (…) '
2 My classmates said that they hadn't believed the story. 'We (…) '
3 My local shopkeeper said that I could buy the product there. 'You (…) '
4 My sister said that she would never buy it. 'I (…) '

6 Read the survey questions. Write short answers that are true for you.

MEDIA SURVEY

1 Do you watch the news on TV?
2 Are you reading any books at the moment?
3 Will you work in the media in the future?
4 Have you ever written a blog?

7 💬 Work in pairs. Ask your partner the questions in exercise 6. Write their answers and then report them to the class.

8 Answer the question to solve the Brain teaser.

Carson Cool said that he was planning to marry Sadie Sharp and that the wedding would be before his birthday (1 September). 'We want a big wedding with all our friends and family,' said the star. Cool's manager told reporters that the star would be on tour in June and July and that he wouldn't have any free days. Cool's mother tweeted that her son's favourite number was 12.

What is the most likely date for the wedding?

Vocabulary and Listening 8

Reporting verbs

1 Read the text and check the meaning of the verbs in bold. Was there a lizard under the bed?

Sock horror! There's a lizard under the bed!

A 'terrified' family called the animal charity RSPCA when they thought there was a dangerous lizard in their house. They **explained** that the pink and brown creature was hiding under their teenage daughter's bed. RSPCA officer Vic Hurr **agreed** to visit their home in Coventry, UK. She **offered** to remove the creature – but soon realised that it was just a dirty sock!

The teenage daughter **admitted** that she hadn't cleaned her room for a while, and **promised** to look after her socks better. Ms Hurr **advised** her to tidy her room more often, and **suggested** that she should look for another 'creature' as they usually come in pairs!

2 Complete 1–5 in the table with the bold verbs in exercise 1. Look carefully at how the verbs are used in the article.

Verb patterns		
v + that	v + to	v + object + to
explain that	agree to	1 (…)
2 (…)	3 (…)	ask (someone) to
4 (…)	5 (…)	invite (someone) to
say that	refuse to	tell (someone) to

3 Choose the correct answers.
1 Our teacher said (…) read the article.
   a to   **b** us to   **c** that we should
2 We promised (…) our homework.
   a do   **b** to do   **c** doing
3 My friend invited (…) go to her birthday party.
   a to   **b** us to   **c** that we should
4 I explained (…) busy.
   a her that I was   **b** that I was   **c** to be

A radio news bulletin

4 🔊 54 Listen to a radio news bulletin. Which four types of news do you hear?
- an international news story
- sports news
- a national news story
- entertainment news
- a local news story

▶ **Subskill: Guessing meaning from context**

You don't need to understand every word. But if there's an important word you don't know, try to guess its meaning from the context.

5 Listen again. Guess the meaning of the words by listening to the context of the news stories.
1 survey   4 heatwave
2 citizen   5 hosts
3 meteorologists   6 equestrian events

6 Listen again. Answer the questions.
1 According to the World Happiness Report, what are the three happiest countries in the world?
2 How many people live in Finland?
3 What three pieces of advice are given to help people stay safe during the hot weather?
4 Why is the heatwave good for supermarkets?
5 Which city will host the Olympic Games in 2028?
6 Have the Olympic Games been in Paris before?

7 💬 Do you ever listen to the radio? If so, which stations?

8 Grammar

Reported offers, requests, suggestions and commands

1 Read the examples and match 1–5 with a–d.

> **Reported offers, requests, suggestions and commands**
>
> 1 'Please rate your happiness levels,' they said.
>   > They asked people to rate their happiness levels.
> 2 'Drink plenty of water!' they said.
>   > They told people to drink plenty of water.
> 3 'Don't sunbathe between 12 and 3!' they said.
>   > They told people not to sunbathe between 12 and 3.
> 4 'We'll wait until 2028,' said Los Angeles.
>   > Los Angeles offered to wait until 2028.
> 5 'You should tidy your room more often,' said Vic.
>   > Vic suggested that she tidy her room more often.

a offers   b requests
c suggestions   d commands

2 Study the examples in exercise 1 again and choose the correct words in rules 1–5.

1 In reported requests, we use **ask/tell** + object + (not) to + infinitive.
2 In reported commands, we use **ask/tell** + object + (not) to + infinitive.
3 We **use/don't use** an object after the verb *offer*.
4 We report suggestions with the verb *suggest* + **to/that**.
5 We **change/don't change** personal pronouns and possessive adjectives in reported offers, requests, suggestions and commands.

3 Choose the correct words to complete the dialogue.

> I was on TV yesterday!
>
> Really? Why?
>
> They **1 asked / told** me to do an interview on the local news. They asked **2 me to / that I** talk about my voluntary work.
>
> That's great! Did they offer **3 to pay you / you to pay**?
>
> They did, actually – but I told them **4 don't / not to** worry about that. They **5 offered / told** to make a donation to the charity instead.
>
> Great!
>
> Yes – I suggested that people **6 look / to look** at the website. Perhaps we'll get some new volunteers!

4 Complete the reported offers, requests, suggestions and commands.

1 'I'll pay for the tickets!' She offered (…)
2 'Put your phones on silent!' They told (…)
3 'Please come for an interview next Monday.' They asked (…)
4 'Why don't you call me later?' He suggested (…)
5 'Don't tell anyone your password!' They told (…)

5 Look at the notes and messages. Then write a reported offer, request, suggestion or command for each one.

Dad told me not to be late.

> Don't be late!
> Dad

> Could you help me with the computer?
> Grandma

> We'll take you out for your birthday!
> Aunt Jane and Uncle Sam

> You must call me a.s.a.p.! Paula

> How about getting the bus to my house?
> Jake

6 Choose the correct options.

GRAMMAR ROUND-UP
1 2 3 4 5 6 7 8

Usain Bolt: from track to pitch

Olympic athletics champion Usain Bolt **1 makes / has made / was making** his football debut for Australian team Central Coast Mariners. About 10,000 fans watched the Jamaican sprinter when he **2 brought / is brought / was brought** on as a substitute towards the end of the 6–1 win. After **3 play / to play / playing** for about 20 minutes, Bolt almost scored. He **4 said / told / told to** reporters that he **5 is / was / has been** 'in good shape', and asked his coach **6 give / to give / giving** him four months to get fit. Bolt **7 has dreamed / had dreamed / was dreaming** of playing football professionally before he went on to win eight Olympic gold medals. Perhaps soon his dream **8 is coming / will come / will be coming** true!

Research
Find out what happened next in Usain Bolt's career.

Reacting to news

1 🎥 Watch the video. Complete 1–4 with words in the box. There are two words you don't need.

> American   Arsenal   Australian
> Chelsea   phone   radio

2 Watch again and answer the questions.
1 Where had Logan's sister heard the news?
2 Why didn't Mae believe him?
3 What did they do to check?

3 Watch again. Which Key phrases show doubt?

Logan: Did you hear the news about Usain Bolt?
Mae: No, what happened?
Logan: Apparently he's playing for 1 (…) .
Mae: That's crazy! Are you sure it's true?
Logan: My sister told me that she'd heard it on the 2 (…) .
Mae: No way, that can't be true!
Logan: That's what she said.
Mae: I think she must have misheard. Are you sure she didn't say an 3 (…) team?
Logan: Oh, maybe. Yes, you might be right.
Mae: Hmm – I think that's more likely.
Logan: Let's Google it and check!
Mae: Yes, good idea. I'll have a look on my 4 (…) .

Real-world speaking

4 Create your own dialogue. Follow the steps in the Skills boost.

> Mo Farah to play for England?

> Tornado sweeps through Madrid.

SKILLS BOOST

THINK
Choose your news topic and make notes about it.

PREPARE
Prepare a dialogue. Remember to include phrases for reacting to news.

PRACTISE
Practise your dialogue. Remember to use appropriate intonation for expressing doubt.

PERFORM
Act out your dialogue for the class.

5 **Peer review** Listen to your classmates. Answer the questions.
1 What news did they talk about?
2 Which Key phrases did they use?
3 Did they use intonation to express doubt?

Key phrases
Did you hear the news about … ?
No, what happened?
Apparently, …
That's crazy/terrible/great! Are you sure it's true?
… told me that he/she had heard it on the radio
No way, that can't be true!
He/she must have misheard/misunderstood.

Real-world grammar
That can't be true!
She must have misheard.
You might be right.

Phrasebook → p125   103

8 Writing

Laugh out Loud!

Pablo Sanchez reports on yesterday's **WORLD LAUGHTER DAY** celebrations

1. World Laughter Day is celebrated every year on the first Sunday of May. ~~Yesterdays~~ celebration here at the park in Pueblo Nuevo is a fun-filled day for all the family.

2. According to organisers, about 3,000 people attended the event. 'It was a huge success, said Ana, one of the volunteers. The day began with a group laughter session, followed by a programme of comedy and live music.

3. Ana explained that World Laughter Day had begun in India in 1998, and that now it was celebrated in more than 100 ~~countrys~~ around the world. Apparently, some studies suggest that group laughter promotes well-being for the whole community.

4. When I asked whether ~~would there be~~ a similar event next year, organisers told me that they hoped it would become an annual event. Let's hope so! They added that more information was available on ~~there~~ blog, and photos of yesterday's event would soon be uploaded on social media.

A news report

1 Read Pablo's report. Did he enjoy the event? How do you know?

2 Match questions a–h with paragraphs 1–4 in Pablo's report. (There are two questions for each paragraph.)
   a How many people attended the event?
   b What is the background to the event?
   c When was the event held?
   d Is more information available?
   e Where was the event?
   f What activities were there?
   g Why is the event held?
   h Will the event be held again?

3 Answer the questions in exercise 2.

▶ Subskill: Editing your writing

Always check your work for errors of: grammar (e.g. tenses, word order), spelling (e.g. plurals, words that sound the same), punctuation (e.g. speech marks, apostrophes).

4 Read the subskill information and identify each type of error in Pablo's report. Then correct the errors.

5 Find and correct six errors in the text about World Bicycle Day. What type of error is each one?

World Bicycle Day was celebrated last weekend in my town, on 3 June. According to organisers, the event was a great success. There is a mass bike ride in the morning and all the roads were closed to traffic. Cycling has social, economic and environmental benefits for all communitys,' explained one of the organisers. I asked if had they plans for other similar events, and they told me that they hoped to keep the roads car-free on other Sunday mornings to. Lets hope so!

6 Write a news report about a local event. Follow the steps in the Skills boost.

SKILLS BOOST

THINK
1 Choose an event that happened recently at your school or in your town/region, or invent one if you prefer!
2 Answer the questions in exercise 2 about your event. Make notes.

PREPARE
Organise your notes into four paragraphs:
1 When? / Where?
2 Who? / What?
3 Background / Why?
4 More info / Future?

WRITE
Write your report. Use the model to help you.

CHECK
Read your report and answer the questions.
1 Have you used direct and reported speech?
2 Have you included vocabulary for news and reporting verbs?
3 Have you written four paragraphs?
4 Have you edited your work?

7 **Peer review** Exchange your report with another student. Answer the questions.
1 How many examples of reported speech can you find? What would the direct speech be?
2 Does the writer make this event sound interesting? Would you like to go?
3 Has he/she edited the report? Can you find any errors?

QUICK REVIEW 8

Grammar

Reported speech
We use reported speech to report what someone said.
'Fresh mountain air **improves** exam results.'
→ The reporter said that fresh mountain air **improved** exam results.

Tense changes

direct speech →	reported speech
present simple	past simple
present continuous	past continuous
past simple	past perfect
present perfect	past perfect
future with *will*	would
can	could

Reported speech: other changes
'**We**'ll send **you** a free gift if you order before **tomorrow**,' said Kidding. → Kidding said that **they** would send **us** a free gift if we ordered before **the following day**.
'I bottle it **here** in **my** garden,' said Kidding. → Kidding said that **he** bottled it **there** in **his** garden.
In reported speech we also change:
subject and object pronouns, possessive adjectives, time expressions, adverbs of place

Reported offers, requests, suggestions and commands
'Please rate your happiness levels,' they said. →
They **asked** people **to rate** their happiness levels.
'Drink plenty of water!' they said. →
They **told** people **to drink** plenty of water.
'Don't sunbathe between 12 and 3!' they said. →
They **told** people **not to sunbathe** between 12 and 3.
'We'll wait until 2028,' said Los Angeles. →
Los Angeles **offered to wait** until 2028.
'You should tidy your room more often,' said Vic Hurr. →
Vic Hurr **suggested that she tidy** her room more often.

Vocabulary

🔊 55 **Types of media**
Broadcast media: radio, TV
Print media: magazines, newspaper
Digital media: blog, podcast, pop-up ads, satellite TV, social media, website

🔊 56 **The news** blogger, broadcast, headlines, interviewee, interviewer, journalism, mass media, newsreader, reliable, reporter, shocking, source, tabloid, trust

🔊 57 **Reporting verbs** admit that, advise (someone) to, agree to, ask (someone) to, explain that, invite (someone) to, offer to, promise to, refuse to, say that, suggest that, tell (someone) to

8 Project

How do we know if news is reliable?

TASK: Report a news story in two different ways: one based on facts and the other based on opinions.

Learning outcomes
1 I can understand how the same information can be presented in different ways.
2 I can use appropriate language from the unit.
3 I can use critical thinking to assess the reliability of sources.

Graphic organiser → Project planner p121

1 🎥 Watch a video of two students presenting their news stories. How does their intonation change?

STEP 1: THINK ◉◯◯◯

2 Work in pairs. Read the articles in the Model Project. Then discuss the questions.
   1 Do the two articles report the same story?
   2 What is the story about?
   3 How are the two articles different?

3 Work in pairs. Look at the articles again. In which article can you find examples of:
   • specific facts?
   • reliable sources?
   • adjectives of opinion?
   • unreliable sources?

STEP 2: PLAN ◉◉◯◯

4 Work in pairs. Follow the instructions.
   1 Choose a news story in one of the categories:
      • entertainment
      • national news
      • sport
      • international news
   2 Decide whether to create a written article or create a news video.

5 Work in pairs. Read the tips in the Super skills box and practise saying the Key phrases with a partner.

CRITICAL THINKING

Assessing the reliability of sources

Tips
Is the author subjective or objective?
Does the source contain facts or opinions?

Key phrases
Have you checked this fact on a different website?
Does the website seem like a reliable source?
This article contains a lot of facts/opinions.
This article lists its sources clearly.
This website seems unreliable.

---

6 Work in pairs. Research the news story you chose in exercise 4. Make notes. Use the tips and Key phrases in the Super skills box.

STEP 3: CREATE ◉◉◉◯

7 Read the *How to …* tips on p121 and create your news articles.

8 Edit your news stories. Check you have used appropriate language from the unit.

106 Grammar and Vocabulary → Quick review p105

Model project

A

Five arrested for orange theft

Five people have been arrested on suspicion of stealing 4,000 kilograms of oranges near Seville, Spain. Two vehicles were stopped by police and a third vehicle was found later. All three vehicles contained large quantities of oranges, which the occupants said they had found on the ground and intended to use for 'personal consumption'. According to police, workers near the port of Carmona had reported the disappearance of a cargo of fruit several hours before.

B

Marmalade madness or criminal cover-up?

Police in Seville have arrested a group of thieves after they tried to escape in the middle of the night. A witness told reporters that when police ordered the crazy criminals to get out of their cars, millions of oranges fell out of the vehicles. When asked why their cars were full of oranges, they told police that they had found them next to the road 'far away' and intended to make jars of marmalade. According to trusted sources, the thieves were intending to make a fortune by selling the fruit (which had a market value in excess of €1,400) to innocent consumers. It has also been suggested that this was a cover-up to distract police from a more serious crime.

STEP 4: PRESENT ●●●●

9 Practise presenting your news stories. Record yourselves and make any necessary changes.

10 Present your news stories to the class.

11 **Peer review** Answer questions from your classmates.

8 FINAL REFLECTION

1 **The task**
How successful were your news stories?
How difficult was it to produce them in two different ways?

2 **Super skills**
Did you assess the reliability of sources using Critical Thinking skills?

3 **Language**
What new language did you use from this unit?

Beyond the task
Why do different sources present news stories in different ways? Think about the emotional effect on the reader/viewer.

9 Look what you know!

1 W (…) (…) (…) E C (…) (…) (…) (…) (…) (…) R C (…) (…) E

2 CR (…) (…) (…) E AN I (…) V (…) (…) T (…) (…) N

3 SE (…) F (…) (…)

4 ST (…) (…) (…) A CA (…) (…) (…) (…) (…) N

5 BE O (…) Y (…) (…) (…) T (…) (…) (…) (…) LS

6 N (…) (…)SR (…) (…) (…) R

7 H (…) (…) E S (…) (…) (…) (…) Y SN (…) (…) (…) S

8 UP (…) (…) (…) D A P (…) (…) (…) O

Vocabulary

1 Look at the photos and complete the words.

2 Match answers (1–8) from exercise 1 to the vocabulary sets (a–h).
  a Helping others (Unit 1)
  b Skills and abilities (Unit 2)
  c Health and well-being (Unit 3)
  d Inventions (Unit 4)
  e Photography (Unit 5)
  f Travelling (Unit 6)
  g Technology (Unit 7)
  h Media and news (Unit 8)

3 Which word or expression does *not* belong in each vocabulary set? Why?
  1 watch video tutorials, revise for a test, record yourself, ride a bike
  2 shock, promise, complain, announce
  3 delicious, small, unforgettable, freezing
  4 graffiti art, abstract, printmaking, photography
  5 cut down on, take care of, set off, talk through
  6 wearable, handy, high quality, rich
  7 follow instructions, change society, win an award, make a difference
  8 print out, sign out, check in, log on

4 Add at least three more words to each group in exercise 3. Which unit are they in?

5 Choose the correct answers to complete the text.

A surprised driver had an 1 (…) journey to work this morning. When Ben Peters, 34, set 2 (…), he didn't expect to see an unusual vehicle – a bumper car! Peters 3 (…) a video of it on his company's Facebook page. In the video, the 4 (…) driver can be seen waiting to turn right. Bumper cars usually need to be connected to an electricity supply so perhaps the driver has created a new 5 (…) ! Meanwhile, another inventor, Mark Harper 6 (…) to journalists how he had adapted a bumper car using an old engine. It isn't too 7 (…) as it has a top speed of 8 miles per hour. However, Mr Harper has 8 (…) the authorities if he can officially use it on the roads.

1 a exhausted b awful   c unforgettable
2 a up   b off   c on
3 a shared   b filmed   c edited
4 a shy   b patient   c enthusiastic
5 a discovery b invention   c solution
6 a complained b convinced   c explained
7 a wearable   b practical   c expensive
8 a asked   b told   c suggested

Look what you know! 9

Reading and critical thinking

1 Look back at the Reading subskills in Units 1–8. Which ones do you think are most useful to help you read the text?

2 Look at the text. Where is it from? Explain your answer.

> a blog   a news website   a reference book

3 🔊 58 Look at the photos and headlines. Match the texts 1–4 with the topics a–d and explain your answers. Then read the texts quickly and check.

- a something that will happen in the future
- b someone who takes photos of people
- c an unusual form of transport
- d someone who is helping people who can't walk

4 Are the sentences true or false? Correct the false sentences.
1. Rachel Wallach knows what it is like to use a wheelchair.
2. All Disrupt Disability wheelchairs have the same seat.
3. Nic Tullis likes taking selfies with his phone.
4. Nic wants people to know about the problem of homeless people.
5. The car company Bugatti built the car with Lego pieces.
6. The car contains over 2,000 motors so it can travel fast.
7. Yusaku Maezawa plans to ask some artists to go on a trip to the moon with him.
8. The artists have to create works of art before the trip into space.

5 **Word work** The words in bold in the texts all appeared in the Word work exercises in Units 1–8. Can you remember what they mean? If not, look back and check!

6 💬 Order the stories from most to least interesting. Compare with a partner. Did you choose the same order? If not, explain your reasons.

What's in the news?

1 Invention changes lives

Entrepreneur Rachel Wallach is **determined** to **improve** life for wheelchair users. Rachel knows from personal experience that it's hard to find a wheelchair that suits your lifestyle – she broke her back when she was 18 and has used a wheelchair since then. Now, her company, Disrupt Disability, uses 3D printing and bicycle technology to make adaptable wheelchairs. You can change the seat, wheels and other parts depending on what you use the chair for, so you can even travel on sand or snow!

2 Social media for social change?

Can photos make a difference to people's lives? Nic Tullis believes they can. Instead of taking selfies with his smartphone like most teens, he started a campaign. The 19-year-old regularly posted photos on Instagram of homeless people in his hometown of St Louis, USA. He had around 4,000 followers and hoped that his photos would **raise** awareness of the problem and inspire others to help. He also organised an exhibition of his photos to raise money for a place where homeless people can stay.

3 No, it's not a toy!

A team of Lego specialists has made an amazing life-sized model of a Bugatti Chiron sports car – with Lego! Over 1 million pieces were used to create the car and it took 13,438 hours to build. Some 2,304 Lego motors **generate** its engine power. Andy Wallace, a professional race car driver, tested it out. Before you are **tempted** to build one, you might like to know its top speed is 29 kilometres per hour!

4 Tourism among the stars

Japanese billionaire Yusaku Maezawa will be the first passenger to fly round the moon with SpaceX. Maezawa loves art and said he would invite 6–8 artists from different countries to travel with him on the flight. After returning from the trip, the artists would create works of art. 'These masterpieces will inspire the dreamer within us all,' Maezawa told the BBC. SpaceX is planning the trip for 2023.

9 Look what you know!

Grammar

Units 1 and 2

1 Choose the correct tense.
1. I was tired so I **didn't go**/**wasn't going** out last night.
2. **Did you ever listen**/**Have you ever listened** to a podcast?
3. Daniel arrived while I **watched**/**was watching** a film. We saw the end together.
4. We **were riding**/**have ridden** in a balloon when we saw the elephants below.
5. I **enjoyed**/**have enjoyed** drawing since I was a child.
6. What were you doing when I **rang**/**was ringing** you?

2 Complete the dialogue with the correct form of the verbs in brackets. Use the past simple, past continuous or present perfect.

> Hi Sam. **1** (…) **(you/have)** a good weekend?

> Yeah! On Saturday I **2** (…) **(go)** climbing. I **3** (…) **(just/start)** lessons on a climbing wall.

> I **4** (…) **(never/go)** climbing. I'd love to try it.

> You should come! Anyway, guess what **5** (…) **(happen)**?

> What?

> I **6** (…) **(leave)** when I saw Gwen Moffat. She's a famous climber!

> What **7** (…) **(she/do)** there?

> She **8** (…) **(be)** there to give a talk about climbing so I stayed to listen to her.

3 Read about three friends and then complete the questions for the answers given. Use the correct form of the word in brackets. Write at least two more questions and answers.

> Jack helped Jill.   Jill helped Tom.   Tom helped Jack.

1. Who (…) ? (Jack)
   Tom did.
2. Who (…) ? (Tom)
   He helped Jack.
3. What (…) ? (do)
   She helped Tom.
4. What (…) ? (happen)
   Three friends helped each other.

Units 3 and 4

1 Complete the sentences so they are true for you.
1. At school, we must …
2. Yesterday I had to …
3. At home, I don't have to …
4. At school, students mustn't …
5. When I was younger, I didn't have to …
6. The right food can help me …
7. Last week I couldn't … because …
8. I was happy/sad when I was/wasn't able to …

2 Complete the sentences with the correct form of the verbs in brackets. Then answer the questions.
1. Did you go to any shops (…) **(buy)** clothes last weekend?
2. In your opinion, is it important (…) **(exercise)** every day?
3. Are you interested in (…) **(join)** a gym?
4. (…) **(skip)** breakfast isn't a good idea. Do you agree?
5. What time did you finish (…) **(do)** your homework yesterday?
6. What do you want (…) **(do)** tonight?

3 Choose the correct option.

Is the United Kingdom the place **1 which/where** football comes from? Many British people would like to think so, but similar ball games **2 existed/had existed** in other countries hundreds of years ago. In 5th-century Japan, people played a ball game **3 which/when** was called kemari. Players **4 stood/had stood** in a circle passing the ball and trying to keep it off the ground. Earlier, people **5 played/had played** a similar game called cuju in China. Cuju teams had up to 16 players **6 who/whose** tried to score goals. However, people first **7 played/had played** modern football in the 1100s – in England!

Look what you know! 9

Units 5 and 6

1 Choose the correct options.

Millions of selfies **1 take/are taken** every year and people **2 love/are loved** seeing them. But what about in the past? Some artists painted self-portraits – Vincent van Gogh was famous for his. He **3 painted/was painted** over 30 of them. Why? He wanted to paint better portraits, but models **4 paid/were paid** and van Gogh didn't have enough money, so he **5 started/was started** painting himself. His last self-portrait **6 painted/was painted** in 1889 and he died in 1890. In 1998 one of his self-portraits **7 bought/was bought** for US$71.5 million. It is one of the most expensive self-portraits ever!

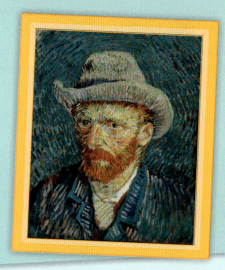

2 Write questions about the text in exercise 1. Use active and passive forms. Then answer the questions.

1 how many / selfies / take / every year ?
2 how many / self-portraits / van Gogh / paint ?
3 why / he / start / painting / self-portraits ?
4 his last self-portrait / paint / in 1890 ?
5 when / he / die ?
6 how much / his last self-portrait / buy for ?

3 Complete the sentences with future forms so they are true for you.

1 Next weekend I'm going to …
2 In the future I might …
3 At this time tomorrow I will be …
4 I think I'll … next year.
5 I probably won't …
6 At nine o'clock this evening I'll be …
7 My first class starts at … tomorrow.
8 I'm meeting …

Units 7 and 8

1 Complete the questions with the correct form of the verb in brackets. Then answer the questions.

1 If you (…) (**have**) a million pounds, would you buy something or save it?
2 If it (…) (**be**) sunny tomorrow, what will you do?
3 If you (…) (**see**) a famous person, what would you do?
4 Where (…) (**you/go**) if you could visit any country in the world?
5 If you (…) (**you/be**) born in the past, when would you have liked to live?
6 (…) (**you/tell**) anyone else if your friend told you a secret?

2 Rewrite the sentences using reported speech.

1 'We're playing basketball tomorrow,' John said.
 John said that (…) .
2 'The government has improved education this year,' a politician said.
 A politician claimed (…) .
3 'I'll phone you later,' Kate said to me.
 Kate told (…) .
4 'My sister can help you,' he said to me.
 He said that (…) .
5 'They created the website last month,' she said.
 She explained that (…) .
6 'We will do our homework,' the students said to the teacher.
 The students promised (…) .

3 Write the sentences in reported speech, using the correct form of the word in brackets.

1 'I'll help you,' she said. (**offer**)
2 'Why don't we go to the cinema?' he said. (**suggest**)
3 'I won't help,' he said. (**refuse**)
4 'Would you like to come to my party?' she said to us. (**invite**)
5 'I won't do it again,' she said. (**promise**)
6 'You're right,' he said to me. (**agree**)

9 Look what you know!

Listening

1 Look back at the Listening subskills in Units 1–8. Which do you find most useful? Why?

2 You are going to listen to four short news stories. Before you listen, look at the photos and answer the questions.
1 What do you think each news story is about?
2 What words or phrases do you think you will hear?

3 🔊 59 Listen to the extracts and check your answers to exercise 2.

4 Listen again and complete the sentences.
1 The University of the People offers low-cost courses to help people get (…).
2 The university now has students in over (…) countries.
3 Marc Treanor creates sand circles on (…) in Wales.
4 On Marc's website you can buy photos and (…) of his work.
5 More and more (…) are teaching students mindfulness.
6 Students who learn mindfulness say they feel less (…).
7 Joelle's campaign to get a celebrity to visit her café lasted (…) days.

5 🔊 60 Read the questions and underline the key words. Then listen to the full story of Joelle's campaign and choose the correct answer. Listen again and check your answers.
1 Joelle wanted
   a to meet a famous actor at the film festival.
   b a famous actor to visit her café.
   c a celebrity to comment on her Twitter posts.
2 Joelle
   a went to see Gosling's film *First Man* at the film festival.
   b thought the film *First Man* would win at the festival.
   c hoped Gosling would attend the film festival in Toronto.
3 Joelle … on Twitter.
   a posted lots of photos of the life-sized Ryan Gosling
   b posted photos of the cardboard Ryan Gosling, but no comments
   c posted only one photo, but lots of comments
4 Joelle's campaign on social media
   a wasn't seen by many people.
   b didn't appear in any other media.
   c became very popular quickly.
5 In the end, Ryan Gosling
   a visited Joelle's café.
   b apologised for not being able to visit.
   c didn't take the time to visit the café.

6 💬 Answer in pairs.
1 Which story did you think was most/least interesting? Why?
2 What surprised you most? Why?

112

Look what you know! 9

Real-world speaking

1 Look at the photos. What phrases do you remember for each situation? Copy and complete the table.

1 Giving an opinion *I thought it was awesome!*	2 Asking for information	3 Checking information (about an event)
4 Talking about photos	5 Giving advice	6 Reacting to news

2 Match a question from A with a response in B and add them to the table in exercise 1.

A
1 Do I need to sign up now?
2 Are you sure it's true?
3 We don't need to buy tickets, do we?
4 What should I do?
5 What did you think?
6 Where was this one taken?

B
a No, it's free.
b It was taken at the beach in Spain.
c I thought it was awesome!
d Yes, that would be best.
e Yes, my brother said he read it online.
f If I were you, I'd talk to your friend about it.

3 🔊 61 Complete the dialogues with one word for each gap. Then listen and check.

1
Antonio: Hi, I'm **1** (…) for information about a coding class. Is it on Thursday?
Receptionist: Yes, at 4:30. Do you want to register?
Antonio: Yes. I've got one more **2** (…) . What time does it finish?
Receptionist: At 5:30.
Antonio: Great. Thanks for your **3** (…) .

2
Alice: Let's make a vegetable omelette. First, get the **4** (…) .
Michael: OK, I've got mushrooms, peppers and eggs, of course.
Alice: Right, you **5** (…) the mushrooms and peppers into pieces.
Michael: OK. What next?
Alice: You need to **6** (…) the vegetables in the pan until they're soft.

3
Zoe: Did you hear the **7** (…) about Sam?
Matilda: No, what happened?
Zoe: **8** (…) , he won a tennis competition!
Matilda: That's crazy! I didn't know he played tennis.

4 Create your own dialogue. Follow the steps in the Skills boost.

SKILLS BOOST

THINK
Choose a situation and make notes.
• You and a friend both went to a theme park. Talk about your opinions of it.
• You want to go camping with some friends. Your parents have said 'no'. Ask a friend for advice.

PREPARE
Prepare a dialogue. Remember to include relevant Key phrases.

WRITE
Practise your dialogue.

CHECK
Act out your dialogue for the class or record it and play it to the class.

5 **Peer review** Listen to your classmates and answer the questions.
1 Which task did they do?
2 Which Key phrases did they use?
3 Could they improve their dialogue? How?

9 Look what you know!

Writing

1 Read the texts quickly. Match texts 1–8 with descriptions a–h. Which unit was each writing genre in?

- a A profile
- b A blog
- c An informal email
- d A formal letter
- e An online post comparing artworks
- f An opinion essay
- g A report of a survey
- h A news report

1

| Register | FAQ | New Posts | Community |

In the foreground, there are figures in both paintings, but you can't see the faces. Both paintings use the colour blue to create a mysterious atmosphere.

2
The most popular social media sites are Snapchat (49%), YouTube (32%) and Instagram (15%). Everyone said that they used social media at least once a week.

3
Hi David,

How are you? Sorry I haven't written for ages! Anyway, I'm writing to see if you want to come to a cycling event that I'm going to.

4
| HOME | ABOUT | BLOG | CONTACT |

What are you working on now?
At the moment I'm learning how to juggle with four balls. I've just learnt a new routine.

How did you get inspired?
I saw a juggler in a circus last year and I tried it. Ever since then, I've loved juggling.

5
World Chocolate Day is celebrated every year on 7th July. Yesterdays celebration in our town is a fun-filled day for all the family.

6
Thank you for considering my application. I would be happy to attend an interview at any time. Please contact me on the number or email above if you require any further information.

7
I admire footballer Phil Foden for many reasons. I think he is enthusiastic and hard-working. Although he is only a teenager, he has already achieved a lot.

8
In conclusion, I believe that that although virtual travel is interesting, it is far better to visit places in person. I'll soon be planning my next trip!

2 Find the words or features in the texts.
1. *now*, *at the moment*, *just*: What tenses do you use with these time expressions? What other tenses and time expressions do you know? (Unit 2)
2. three formal expressions: What other formal expressions can you remember? (Unit 4)
3. *although*: What is the difference between *because*, *so* and *although*? (Unit 1)
4. *I believe*: What other expressions do you know for giving opinions? (Unit 6)
5. *a mistake*: What other errors should you check for when you edit your work? (Unit 8)
6. *both*: What is the difference between *both* and *neither*? Where do they go in a sentence? (Unit 5)
7. *everyone*: What other indefinite pronouns are there? (Unit 7)
8. three different punctuation marks: What are the punctuation marks? What are they used for? (Unit 3)

3 Choose a task and write your answer.

| Task A: You have just learnt a new skill or sport. Write a blog about it. |
| Task B: 'It is better to travel alone than with friends or family.' Do you agree or disagree? |

SKILLS BOOST

THINK
1. Decide which task to do and make notes.
2. Look through the book and find useful language.

PREPARE
1. Organise your writing.
2. Think about the format of your text. Look back at the writing tasks to help you.

WRITE
Write your blog or opinion essay.

CHECK
Read your writing.
1. Did you use correct grammar, spelling and punctuation?
2. Did you use a range of vocabulary and appropriate connectors and phrases?

4 **Peer review** Work in pairs. Read your partner's writing.
1. Which task did your partner do?
2. Are the grammar, vocabulary and punctuation correct?
3. Make one suggestion to improve the writing.

Review game

Look what you know! 9

1. What are blueberries and bananas good for?

2. Where is the ArcelorMittal Orbit slide?

3. When is World Laughter Day?

4. What is geotagging and why could it cause you problems?

5. Zoella is famous for being a beauty vlogger, but she also launched a campaign for an organisation. What is the campaign for? What is the organisation?

6. What did Anurudh Ganesan invent?
   a an ecological bike
   b a way of transporting vaccines
   c a bike that helps you get fit

7. What is Natalie Hampton's app called and what is it for?

8. Where did photographer David Slater take a photo of a macaque that went viral?
   a India
   b Indonesia
   c Iraq

9. Who invented the trampoline?

10. Where did Soap for Health start and who started it?

11. Who is Yayoi Kusama and what is she famous for?

12. Bibi the African parrot loves languages. How many languages can she say 'hello' in?
    a 5
    b 10
    c 20

13. Usain Bolt is a famous athlete, but what sport has he retrained for?

14. How many countries is Vedangi Kulkarni going to cycle through?
    a 15
    b 21
    c 36

15. Where can teenagers do a course to learn to drive?

16. What are these water balls called and why are they good for the environment?

Pronunciation

Unit 1

-ed endings: /d/ /t/ /ɪd/

Pronouncing -ed
There are three pronunciations of –ed endings: /d/ /t/ and /ɪd/.

1 🔊 62 Listen to the sounds.

2 🔊 63 Copy and complete the table.

/d/	/t/	/ɪd/
played	finished	wanted

We use the same rules for adjectives that end in –ed.

3 🔊 64 Complete the groups. Then listen, check and repeat.

bored   convinced   determined
disappointed   embarrassed   excited
interested   surprised   relaxed   talented

1 /d/   2 /t/   3 /ɪd/

Silent letters

1 🔊 65 Identify the silent letters in the words in the box. Then listen, check and repeat.

campaign   climb   designer   difference
exciting   favourite   hour   knowledge
listener   walk   write

Unit 2

Recognising contractions

1 🔊 66 Listen and write the four sentences. Are they past simple or present perfect?

2 🔊 67 Listen and repeat the sentences.
   1 a She learnt to drive.   b She's learnt to drive.
   2 a I designed an app.   b I've designed an app.

Unit 3

Short /ɒ/ and long /ɔː/

1 🔊 68 Listen to the two sounds /ɒ/ and /ɔː/. The first sound is short and the second sound is long.

2 🔊 69 Which sound do the words have, /ɒ/ or /ɔː/? Complete the lists. Then listen, check and repeat.

body   four   morning   often
outdoors   sport   stop   water

Unit 4

Diphthongs

Diphthongs are when you pronounce two individual sounds together, for example /a/ and /ɪ/ become /aɪ/.

1 🔊 70 Listen and repeat the sounds.
   /a/ /ɪ/ → /aɪ/   kind
   /e/ /ɪ/ → /eɪ/   play
   /ə/ /ʊ/ → /əʊ/   go
   /ɪ/ /ə/ → /ɪə/   ear

2 🔊 71 Listen and write the words in the table.

brain   chose   create   design   device
engineer   fear   investigate   phone   scientist

/aɪ/ kind	/eɪ/ play	/əʊ/ go	/ɪə/ ear

3 Listen again and repeat the words.

4 🔊 72 Work in pairs. Practise saying the sentences. Listen and check.
   1 The scientist designed a device.
   2 Use your brain to investigate and create.
   3 I chose a phone.
   4 That engineer has no fear.

Pronunciation

Unit 5
Weak forms: /ə/ with *was* /wəz/ and *were* /wə/

1 🔊 73 **Listen to the sentences. Which two have got the weak form *was* /wəz/?**
   1 **a** Was the photo published?
     b Yes, it was.
   2 **a** Where was it taken?
     b It was taken in Indonesia.

2 **Choose the correct words.**
   1 We **use/don't use** the weak forms of *was* and *were* with Wh– questions and full answers.
   2 We **use/don't use** the weak forms of *was* and *were* with Yes/No questions and short answers.

3 🔊 74 **Listen to the sentences and repeat.**

4 **Listen again and write the sentences. Which two have got the weak form of *were* /wə/?**

Unit 6
going to /gənə/

In spoken English, we often pronounce *going to* as *gonna* /gənə/.

1 🔊 75 **Listen and repeat the phrases.**
   1 What are we going to do now?
   2 I'm going to get the bus into town.
   3 Really? You aren't going to go out now, are you?

2 🔊 76 **Listen and write the sentences. Write the full form of *going to*.**

Syllables and word stress with extreme adverbs and adjectives

1 🔊 77 **Listen and repeat the words. Which syllables are stressed?**
   1 ab-so-lute-ly a-ma-zing
   2 real-ly un-for-get-ta-ble
   3 to-tal-ly ex-haus-ted

2 🔊 78 **Listen to eight words and complete the table. Which syllables are stressed?**

2 syllables	3 syllables	4 syllables

Unit 7
Sentence stress

We usually stress the content words in sentences. In conditional sentences we don't usually stress *if*.

1 🔊 79 **Listen to the sentences and notice the stressed words. Notice what happens to the other words.**

If I **upload** it now, my **friends** will see this **photo**.
If I **took** a **selfie** that I didn't **like**, I wouldn't **post** it.
If my **friends** had **helped**, I would have **finished** the **project**.

2 🔊 80 **Choose the words you think are stressed in the sentences. Then listen and check.**
   1 If Kate had time, she would text me.
   2 If we hadn't gone to the party, we wouldn't have met Sam.
   3 If I see Jack, I'll give him the message.

Unit 8
Intonation in reported speech

1 🔊 81 **Listen and repeat the sentences in direct speech. Pay attention to the stressed words.**
   1 I heard it on the radio.
   2 It was a joke!
   3 Listen carefully!

2 🔊 82 **Copy the reported speech. Listen. What do you notice about the words which are stressed?**
   1 She said she'd heard it on the radio.
   2 He admitted that it was a joke.
   3 She told us to listen carefully.

117

Project planner

Unit 1 Graphic organiser

How to make a video
- Write your script.
- Organise your equipment – a smartphone, video camera or web cam.
- Sit facing the light and speak loudly and clearly.
- Watch the recording. What can you improve? If necessary, record it again with improvements.
- Use an editing tool to add music, images and effects.

Unit 2 Graphic organiser

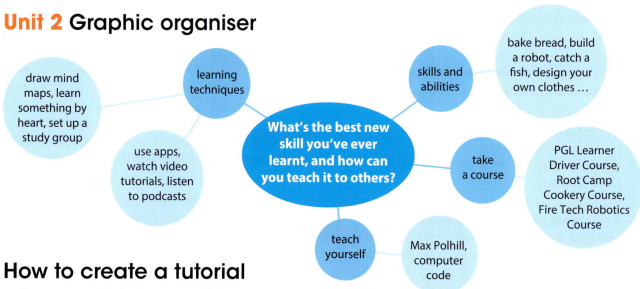

How to create a tutorial
- Choose a specific aim for your tutorial.
- Think about your target audience and choose the best format for your tutorial (video, audio, written or face-to-face?)
- Research similar tutorials online to get some ideas.
- Plan and write your script. Include a title, an introduction, a few steps and a concluding section.
- Include images, video or demonstrations, if appropriate.
- Practise following your tutorial to check that it's easy to understand. Edit if necessary.

Project planner

Unit 3 Graphic organiser

How to plan and create a fitness diary

- List the fitness activities you can do.
- Evaluate the advantages and disadvantages of each idea.
- Plan the number of activities you want to do.
- Decide when you will do the activities.
- Take photos or make a video while you do the activities.
- Review your plan and evaluate how successful you were and why.

Unit 4 Graphic organiser

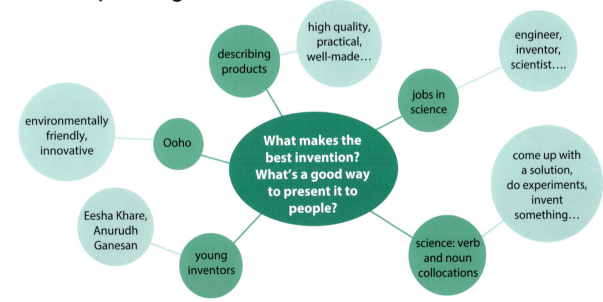

How to give a product pitch

- Decide on the product. Brainstorm:
    - why people need the product
    - who would buy it
    - why it is unique and a good business idea.
- Your pitch should be short and include the most important information. Aim for one minute.
- Include persuasive language in your script.
- Point to your visual material to help your audience understand.
- Use confident body language – clear gestures and good eye contact.
- Be prepared to answer questions.

Project planner

Unit 5 Graphic organiser

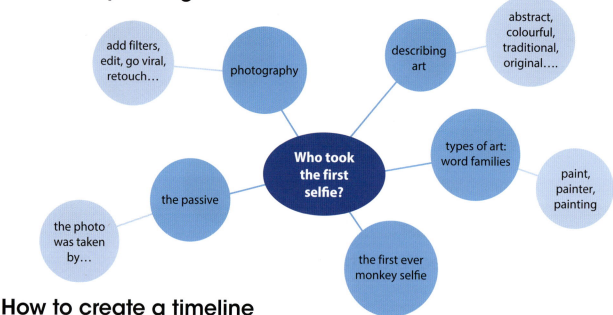

How to create a timeline
- Choose your subject. Select your start and end dates. Research a list of events to include.
- Look at examples of different timelines online. Choose your preferred format (horizontal or vertical).
- Draw your timeline or use a digital template.
- Write about each event separately. Put the events in chronological order.
- Add pictures.
- Add a title. Edit your work before presenting it.

Unit 6 Graphic organiser

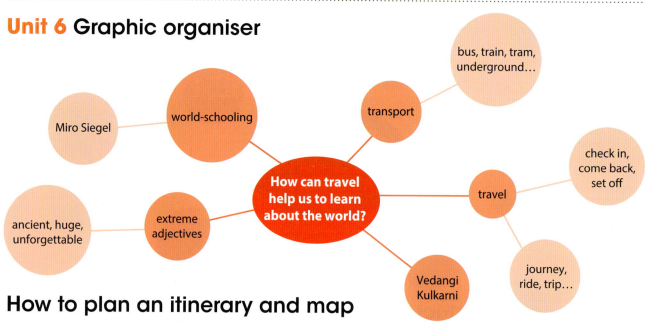

How to plan an itinerary and map
- Brainstorm places that you'd like to visit.
- Research specific information, for example:
  - what you can visit there
  - details of opening times and prices
  - transport and travel time
  - length of the trip.
- Mark all the places you want to visit on a map and choose the best route. Draw a map, or use an interactive map online.
- Use photos of your destinations to make it more interesting.

Project planner

Unit 7 Graphic organiser

How to write a questionnaire

- Decide on your objective. Write down the information you want to find out.
- Write questions to find out the information. Choose the best question type for each question.
- Use clear, simple language.
- Ask one thing at a time.
- Avoid giving too many or too few options.
- Include 'Don't know' or 'Not applicable' as options where relevant.
- Test your questionnaire on one or more people.
- Revise the questionnaire as necessary.

Unit 8 Graphic organiser

How to research and report on a news story

- Use at least three different sources to research.
- Check the reliability of the sources.
- Make notes of the key points – where? when? who? what? how?
- Decide on a style: factual or sensational language?
- Write a headline to match the style.
- Decide whether to present it as an article or a video news report. Plan the introduction, the main body and a conclusion.
- Edit your work before presenting it. Check that the style is consistent.

Phrasebook

Unit 1 Giving an opinion

Asking for and giving opinions

- What do/did you think (of …)?
- Don't/Didn't you think that …?
- What do you reckon?
- I reckon (that) …
- I think …
- I thought …
- I (really) feel that …
- I really felt that …
- In my opinion …
- If you ask me …

> 🗨️ **US → UK** Words from the unit
>
> non profit → charity   She started a non-profit (US) / charity (UK) which provides books for schools in poor areas.

Unit 2 Asking for information

- I'm looking for information about …
- Have you … before?
- I've heard it's very popular.
- Do I need to sign up now?
- I've got one more question.
- Thanks for your help.
- Just ask if you need any more information.

> 🗨️ **US → UK** Words from the unit
>
> review → revise   I have to review (US) / revise (UK) irregular verbs before the test tomorrow.
>
> backpack → rucksack   I always carry a backpack (US) / rucksack (UK) with my school books, my phone and my wallet in it.

Phrasebook

Unit 3 Giving instructions

Sequencing

- First … Next … Then … Finally

Preparing food

- Get/Measure/Add the ingredients.
- Cut/Chop (it/them/the fruit) into pieces.
- Mix/Cook (it/them/the dish) for (2 minutes).
- Pour (it/the mix/the liquid) into (a glass/a pan).
- A cup/teaspoon/tablespoon/handful of (fruit).

 US → UK Words from the unit

kilometers → kilometres   With the jet pack you can travel up to 80 kilometers (US) / kilometres (UK) per hour.

Unit 4 Checking information

Checking about the present

- The light show starts at 6:00 pm, <u>doesn't it?</u>
- We don't need to buy tickets, <u>do we?</u>
- It's on for four nights, <u>isn't it?</u>

Checking about the past

- You checked the route, <u>didn't you?</u>
- We didn't eat there last time, <u>did we?</u>
- There was a lot to see, <u>wasn't there?</u>
- There were a lot of cafés open, <u>weren't there?</u>

 US → UK Words from the unit

stove → cooker   We heated our soup on the stove (US) / cooker (UK).
chips → crisps   Sometimes I have a packet of chips (US) / crisps (UK) as a snack.
fries → chips   The fish comes with fries (US) / chips (UK) and salad.

Phrasebook

Unit 5 Talking about photos

- I saw your (vacation) photos on Instagram.
- Do you want to have a look at the rest?
- This one's amazing/great!
- Where was it taken?
- That one was taken at/in …
- It looks beautiful/so peaceful.
- It looks like …/It looked like …
- I like/love this one/this selfie!

 US → UK Words from the unit

colorful → colourful	These flowers are so colorful (US) / colourful (UK).
vacation → holiday	My family and I usually go to the beach on vacation (US) / holiday (UK).
cell phone → mobile phone	I use my cell phone (US) / mobile phone (UK) for messaging, playing games and listening to music.

Unit 6 Buying tickets

- Can I help you
- Are you travelling now?
- How long does it take?
- Single or return?
- How much is it?
- Are you paying cash or card?

 US → UK Words from the unit

favorite → favourite	Train is my favorite (US) / favourite (UK) way to travel.
subway → underground	The quickest way to travel in London is on the subway (US) / underground (UK).
theater → theatre	I've always wanted to see a Shakespeare play at the theater (US) / theatre (UK).
traveling → travelling	Next summer, my family and I will be traveling (US) / travelling (UK) around Europe.

Phrasebook

Unit 7 Giving advice

Asking for advice

- Can I ask your advice?
- What would you do (if …)?
- How would you feel (if …)?
- What should I do?
- What would you do?

Giving advice

- If I were you, I'd …
- I think you should …
- You should/shouldn't have …
- Why don't you …?
- You could …

 US → UK Words from the unit

soccer → football	My favourite soccer (US) / football (UK) team is Manchester city.
high school → secondary school	Most teenagers study at high school (US) / secondary school (UK).

Unit 8 Reacting to news

- Did you hear the news about … ?
- No, what happened?
- Apparently, …
- That's crazy/terrible/great! Are you sure it's true?
- … told me that he/she had heard it on the radio.
- No way, that can't be true!
- He/she must have misheard/misunderstood.

 US → UK Words from the unit

organize → organise	They organized (US) / organised (UK) an event to celebrate World Laughter Day.
realize → realise	I soon realized (US) / realised (UK) what had happened.

Irregular verbs

Infinitive	Past simple	Past participle
be /biː/	was / were /wɒz/, /wɜː(r)/	been /biːn/
become /bɪˈkʌm/	became /bɪˈkeɪm/	become /bɪˈkʌm/
begin /bɪˈgɪn/	began /bɪˈgæn/	begun /bɪˈgʌn/
bet /bet/	bet /bet/	bet /bet/
break /breɪk/	broke /brəʊk/	broken /ˈbrəʊkən/
bring /brɪŋ/	brought /brɔːt/	brought /brɔːt/
broadcast /ˈbrɔːdˌkɑːst/	broadcast /ˈbrɔːdˌkɑːst/	broadcast /ˈbrɔːdˌkɑːst/
build /bɪld/	built /bɪlt/	built /bɪlt/
buy /baɪ/	bought /bɔːt/	bought /bɔːt/
catch /kætʃ/	caught /kɔːt/	caught /kɔːt/
choose /tʃuːz/	chose /tʃəʊz/	chosen /ˈtʃəʊz(ə)n/
come /kʌm/	came /keɪm/	come /kʌm/
cost /kɒst/	cost /kɒst/	cost /kɒst/
cut /kʌt/	cut /kʌt/	cut /kʌt/
do /duː/	did /dɪd/	done /dʌn/
draw /drɔː/	drew /druː/	drawn /drɔːn/
dream /driːm/	dreamed/dreamt /driːmd//dremt/	dreamed/dreamt /driːmd//dremt/
drink /drɪŋk/	drank /dræŋk/	drunk /drʌŋk/
drive /draɪv/	drove /drəʊv/	driven /ˈdrɪv(ə)n/
eat /iːt/	ate /eɪt/	eaten /ˈiːt(ə)n/
fall /fɔːl/	fell /fel/	fallen /ˈfɔːlən/
feed /fiːd/	fed /fed/	fed /fed/
feel /fiːl/	felt /felt/	felt /felt/
fight /faɪt/	fought /fɔːt/	fought /fɔːt/
find /faɪnd/	found /faʊnd/	found /faʊnd/
fly /flaɪ/	flew /fluː/	flown /fləʊn/
forget /fə(r)ˈget/	forgot /fə(r)ˈgɒt/	forgotten /fə(r)ˈgɒt(ə)n/
get /get/	got /gɒt/	got /gɒt/
give /gɪv/	gave /geɪv/	given /ˈgɪv(ə)n/
go /gəʊ/	went /went/	gone /gɒn/
grow /grəʊ/	grew /gruː/	grown /grəʊn/
hang /hæŋ/	hung /hʌŋ/	hung /hʌŋ/
have /hæv/	had /hæd/	had /hæd/
hear /hɪə(r)/	heard /hɜː(r)d/	heard /hɜː(r)d/
hide /haɪd/	hid /hɪd/	hidden /ˈhɪd(ə)n/
hit /hɪt/	hit /hɪt/	hit /hɪt/

Irregular verbs

Infinitive	Past simple	Past participle
hold /həʊld/	held /held/	held /held/
keep /kiːp/	kept /kept/	kept /kept/
know /nəʊ/	knew /njuː/	known /nəʊn/
lay /leɪ/	laid /leɪd/	laid /leɪd/
learn /lɜː(r)n/	learnt/learned /lɜː(r)nt//lɜː(r)nd/	learnt/learned /lɜː(r)nt//lɜː(r)nd/
leave /liːv/	left /left/	left /left/
let /let/	let /let/	let /let/
lose /luːz/	lost /lɒst/	lost /lɒst/
make /meɪk/	made /meɪd/	made /meɪd/
mean /miːn/	meant /ment/	meant /ment/
meet /miːt/	met /met/	met /met/
pay /peɪ/	paid /peɪd/	paid /peɪd/
put /pʊt/	put /pʊt/	put /pʊt/
read /riːd/	read /red/	read /red/
ride /raɪd/	rode /rəʊd/	ridden /ˈrɪd(ə)n/
ring /rɪŋ/	rang /ræŋ/	rung /rʌŋ/
run /rʌn/	ran /ræn/	run /rʌn/
say /seɪ/	said /sed/	said /sed/
see /siː/	saw /sɔː/	seen /siːn/
sell /sel/	sold /səʊld/	sold /səʊld/
send /send/	sent /sent/	sent /sent/
set /set/	set /set/	set /set/
shine /ʃaɪn/	shone/shined /ʃɒn//ʃaɪnd/	shone/shined /ʃɒn//ʃaɪnd/
show /ʃəʊ/	showed /ʃəʊd/	shown /ʃəʊn/
sing /sɪŋ/	sang /sæŋ/	sung /sʌŋ/
sit /sɪt/	sat /sæt/	sat /sæt/
sleep /sliːp/	slept /slept/	slept /slept/
speak /spiːk/	spoke /spəʊk/	spoken /ˈspəʊkən/
spend /spend/	spent /spent/	spent /spent/
stand /stænd/	stood /stʊd/	stood /stʊd/
steal /stiːl/	stole /stəʊl/	stolen /ˈstəʊlən/
stick /stɪk/	stuck /stʌk/	stuck /stʌk/
sweep /swiːp/	swept /swept/	swept /swept/
swim /swɪm/	swam /swæm/	swum /swʌm/
take /teɪk/	took /tʊk/	taken /ˈteɪkən/
teach /tiːtʃ/	taught /tɔːt/	taught /tɔːt/
tell /tel/	told /təʊld/	told /təʊld/
think /θɪŋk/	thought /θɔːt/	thought /θɔːt/
throw /θrəʊ/	threw /θruː/	thrown /θrəʊn/
understand /ˌʌndə(r)ˈstænd/	understood /ˌʌndə(r)ˈstʊd/	understood /ˌʌndə(r)ˈstʊd/
wake /weɪk/	woke /wəʊk/	woken /ˈwəʊkən/
wear /weə(r)/	wore /wɔː(r)/	worn /wɔː(r)n/
win /wɪn/	won /wʌn/	won /wʌn/
write /raɪt/	wrote /rəʊt/	written /ˈrɪt(ə)n/

Macmillan Education Limited
4 Crinan Street
London N1 9XW

Companies and representatives throughout the world

Get Involved! Student's Book B1 ISBN 978-1-380-06507-0
Get Involved! Student's Book B1 with Student's App and Digital Student's Book
ISBN 978-1-380-06887-3

Text © Gill Holley, Catherine McBeth, Kate Pickering, Patricia Reilly 2021
Design and illustration © Macmillan Education Limited 2021

The authors have asserted their right to be identified as the authors of this work in accordance with the Copyright, Designs and Patents Act 1988.

First published 2021

All rights reserved. No part of this publication may be reproduced, stored in a retrieval system, or transmitted in any form or by any means, electronic, mechanical, photocopying, recording, or otherwise, without the prior written permission of the publishers.

Original design by Designers Educational Ltd and emc design ltd
Page make-up by Wild Apple Design Ltd
Illlustrated by Daniela Geremia (Beehive Illustration) p58; Camille Medina (Beehive Illustration) p31
Cover design by Designers Educational Ltd
Cover illustration/photograph by Getty Images/Andersen Ross Photography Inc, Getty Images/CoffeeAndMilk, Getty Images/Catherine Ledner, Getty Images/Maskot, Getty Images/uschools
Picture research by Sarah Wells
Cover image research by Penelope Bowden, Proudfoot Pictures

Authors' acknowledgements
Catherine McBeth would like to thank everyone around the world who has helped in the creation of this book, and her family and friends for their support.
Patricia Reilly would like to thank all of the team at Macmillan Education for their hard work and dedication to the project. She would also like to thank her family, especially Alisha, who makes everything worthwhile (and makes a great cup of tea!).

The authors and publishers would like to thank the following for permission to reproduce their photographs:
Alamy Stock Photo/Aflo Co., Ltd p80(cr), Alamy Stock Photo/age fotostock p23(cl), Alamy Stock Photo/Aleksandr Kichigin p10(l), Alamy Stock Photo/Andrew Unangst p65(A), Alamy Stock Photo/anita Delimont p63(bl), Alamy Stock Photo/Anna Kucherova p39(bl), Alamy Stock Photo/Antonio Guillem Fernández p90(tl), Alamy Stock Photo/ARCTIC IMAGES p24(e), Alamy Stock Photo/Art Collection 2 p69(r), Alamy Stock Photo/Avpics p59(r), Alamy Stock Photo/Ben Gingell p17(inset, l), Alamy Stock Photo/blickwinkel p6(b), Alamy Stock Photo/bobo p99(b), Alamy Stock Photo/Classic Image p61(E), Alamy Stock Photo/Dennis Hallinan p68(tr), Alamy Stock Photo/Denys Kovtun p60(C), Alamy Stock Photo/Dorling Kindersley Ltd p83(B), Alamy Stock Photo/dpa picture alliance p18(bl), Alamy Stock Photo/Everett Collection Inc. p23(tr), p65(C), Alamy Stock Photo/Granger Historical Picture Archive p111(l), Alamy Stock Photo/History and Art Collection p71(tr), Alamy Stock Photo/Ian Dagnall pp11(5), 65(E), 83(D), Alamy Stock Photo/Ihor Svetiukha p84(1), Alamy Stock Photo/ imageBROKER pp6(tcr), 30(l), Alamy Stock Photo/Iurii Golub p32, Alamy Stock Photo/ Jamie Gladden/Stockimo p79(r), Alamy Stock Photo/Jan Wlodarczyk p72-73(inset background), Alamy Stock Photo/jeremy sutton-hibbert p65(D), Alamy Stock Photo/Jerónimo Alba p65(B), Alamy Stock Photo/ken biggs p72(2), Alamy Stock Photo/LightField Studios Inc. p96(3), Alamy Stock Photo/Lucas Vallecillos p73(3), Alamy Stock Photo/Luke MacGregor p69(l), Alamy Stock Photo/marrakeshh p39(cr), Alamy Stock Photo/MBI p24(D), Alamy Stock Photo/MediaPunch Inc. p67(r), Alamy Stock Photo/Mladen Mitrinovic p89(cl), Alamy Stock Photo/MPSPhotography p51(tl), Alamy Stock Photo/NASA Image Collection p54(cl), Alamy Stock Photo/Nigel Dollentas p9, Alamy Stock Photo/Norbert Buchholz p104(br), Alamy Stock Photo/Panther Media GmbH p89(tr), Alamy Stock Photo/Pavel Stasevich p84(7), Alamy Stock Photo/PhotosIndia.com LLC p6(bl), Alamy Stock Photo/Pictorial Press Ltd p18(br), Alamy Stock Photo/Rafael Ben-Ari p8(tr), Alamy Stock Photo/Roeland Van de Velde p78(br), Alamy Stock Photo/Roy LANGSTAFF p83(1), Alamy Stock Photo/SERGEI CHAIKO p43, Alamy Stock Photo/Sergey Mironov pp24(A), 108(1), Alamy Stock Photo/Shotshop GmbH p71(inset tl), Alamy Stock Photo/SpaceX p109(cr), Alamy Stock Photo/Stephen Chung p15(r), Alamy Stock Photo/Taras Vyshnya p55(r), Alamy Stock Photo/Trinity Mirror/Mirrorpix p110(br), Alamy Stock Photo/Vadym Drobot p111(r), Alamy Stock Photo/Viacheslav Iakobchuk p109(tl), Alamy Stock Photo/VogelSP p99(tc), Alamy Stock Photo/way out west photography pp2(l), 48-49(background), 48(1), Alamy Stock Photo/Zoonar GmbH p44-45(b), Alamy Stock Photo/ZUMA Press, Inc. p14; **Archant Norfolk** p17(t); **BBC Studios Ltd** pp11(3), 12-13; **Bournemouth University**/Jonathan Beal p77; **Bye Bye Plastic Bags** p23(bl), 108(4); **Caters News Agency Ltd/David J Slater** pp11(2), 63(tr), 115(8, and background); **Corbis**/Fuse p101(br); **Daniel Bedell Photography** pp2(cl), 51(bl); **ESA** p13(cn); **FITT360**/LINKFLOW p53(A); **Fooducate** p37(tl); **Getty Images** pp34-35(b), 39(cl), 84(3), Getty Images/AFP/JOHN MACDOUGALL p103(r), 115(13), Getty Images/AFP/PETER PARKS pp11(1), 102, Getty Images/Anadolu Agency p19(r), Getty Images/Art Vandalay p114(4), Getty Images/Bettmann p54(cr), Getty Images/Blend Images/Peathegee Inc. p71(inset tc), Getty Images/Caiaimage/Agnieszka Olek p108(2), Getty Images/Caiaimage/Chris Ryan pp37(br), 44(background, and inset), Getty Images/Charlie Crowhurst/Stringer pp53(tr), 115(16), Getty Images/Chesnot p109(tr), Getty Images/Corbis/Brooke Fasani Auchincloss p36(tr), Getty Images/Corbis/Richard Bailey p89(br), Getty Images/CSA Images p84(2), Getty Images/Cultura RM Exclusive/Albert Lleal Moya p48(5), Getty Images/Cultura/Hybrid Images p7(tcr), Getty Images/Cultura/Lottie Davies p107(b), Getty Images/Cultura/Soren Hald p10(inset), Getty Images/d3sign/Moment p3(br), Getty Images/Digital Vision Vectors/Grafissimo p60(A), Getty Images/Digital Vision Vectors/Vectorios2016 p84(5), Getty Images/Digital Vision/Aaron Foster p80(tr, sky), Getty Images/Digital Vision/Henry Hunt p36(l), Getty Images/Digital Vision/Hill Street Studios pp24(C), 31(r), Getty Images/Digital Vision/Thomas Barwick p47(tr), Getty Images/E+/asiseeit p61(E), Getty Images/E+/fstop123 p27(br), Getty Images/E+/kate_sept2004 p71(cr), Getty Images/E+/LauriPatterson p39(br), Getty Images/E+/Martin-dm pp6(tr), 40, Getty Images/E+/SolStock p36(br), Getty Images/E+/Steve Debenport p7(bc), Getty Images/E+/Subjug p39(tr), Getty Images/E+/tomazl pp96(4), 108(6), Getty Images/EyeEm/Anna Vecher p104(bl), Getty Images/EyeEm/Arisara Tongdonnoi p15(cr), Getty Images/EyeEm/Lisa Norris p24(b), Getty Images/Guerilla p108(3), Getty Images/Hero Images pp24(B), 25(F), 71(inset tr), 110(tl), 112(1), Getty Images/Hultin Archive/Three Lions p8(bcl), Getty Images/Image Source pp41(bl), 85(tl), Getty Images/iStock/AkelSeven p84(4), Getty Images/iStock/alainolympus p114(5), Getty Images/iStock/Amy_Lv p52(cr), Getty Images/iStock/eternalcreative p47(tc), Getty Images/iStock/g-stockstudio p112(3), Getty Images/iStock/gbh007 p47(tl), Getty Images/iStock/I'smail Çiydem p41(cr), Getty Images/iStock/IIIerlok_Xolms pp84(4), 84(8), Getty Images/iStock/Ilyaliren p87(tr), Getty Images/iStock/JackF p7(tr), Getty Images/iStock/Milkos p7(bc), Getty Images/iStock/Ociacia p26, Getty Images/iStock/pixelliebe pp10(emojis), 23(br), 27(emojis), 29, 35(br), 47(br), 59(br), 76, 83(br), 95(br), 107(br), Getty Images/iStock/Rawpixel p81(tl), Getty Images/iStock/themacx pp70-71(background), Getty Images/iStock/Tijana87 p39(tl), Getty Images/iStock/ValentynVolkov p39(tcl), Getty Images/iStock/ViewApart p.92(tl), Getty Images/iStock/Yayayoyo p68(cl), Getty Images/iStockphoto/Thinkstock Images/scanrail p96(1), Getty Images/Jason Todd Photography p70(inset bl), Getty Images/Kevin Lee p73(5), Getty Images/LordRunar p41(tl), Getty Images/Moment/d3sign p2(bc), Getty Images/Moment/DoctorEgg p8(bl), Getty Images/Moment/Elva Etienne p108(7), Getty Images/Moment/Mariano Sayno/Husayno.com p91(r), Getty Images/Moment/Paul Mansfield Photography p6(tcl), Getty Images/Moment/Whitworth Images p72(1), Getty Images/Moment Select/Carlo A p22-23(background), Getty Images/National Geographic Image Collection/Nicolas Reynard p16, Getty Images/Onoky/Eric Audras p70(inset l), Getty Images/Photographer's Choice/Murat Taner p83(C), Getty Images/Stone/Daly and Newton p6-7(tc), Getty Images/Stringer/Matt Cardy p66(b), Getty Images/Stringer/Sean Gallup p71(cl), Getty Images/sturti p108(5), Getty Images/Taxi/Catherine Ledner p104-105(t), Getty Images/Taxi/Tara Moore p37(cr), Getty Images/Tetra images RF/PT Images p70(inset tl), Getty Images/The Image Bank/John Rensten p7(br), Getty Images/The Image Bank/Nick Dolding p47(bl), Getty Images/Vincenzo Lombardo p88(r), Getty Images/Westend61 pp6(5), 27(tr), 27(cr); **Grinder Coffee** p112(4); **Headspace** p37(bc); **Kristian Mensa** pp2(c), 68(cr); **Marc Treanor** p112(2); **Maximillan Polhill** pp28, 28(alien); Moment RF/Carol Yepes p96(6); **Nature Picture Library**/Solvin Zankl p63(br); **Nobody Sits Alone**/Natalie Hampton pp11(4), 90(r); **Pedro Anibarro**/Meal Reminder p37(b); **Project World School** p75(c), 75(r); **Rebecca Constantino** p20(br); **Richard Coyne** p48(3); **Science Photo Library**/DAVID ROBERTSON, ICR p48(4); **Sharon Radisch for Eco-Soap Bank**, 2016 pp2(cr), 2(tl), 115(10); Shutterstock pp11(7), 42(br), 115(5), Shutterstock/Anna Cinaroglu p88(l), Shutterstock/Charnchai Saeheng p25(E), Shutterstock/David Smart p92, Shutterstock/donatas1205 p106-107(background), Shutterstock/EPA/Imas/Jennifer Lavers Handout p8(tcr), Shutterstock/Gal Istvan Gal p96(5), Shutterstock/Gazoukoo p78(doodles), Shutterstock/Jason Winter p58-59(background), Shutterstock/JeDo_Foto p108(8), Shutterstock/jirabu p72(3), Shutterstock/JoeSAPhotos p15(bl), Shutterstock/Kvitka Fabian pp2(tc), 107a, Shutterstock/ lustrous pp104(logo), 115(3), Shutterstock/majcot p53(B), Shutterstock/Nuamfolio p13(background), Shutterstock/Pike-28 p13(tr), Shutterstock/Sasa Prudkov p47(br), Shutterstock/Svetlana Cherruty p46-47(background), Shutterstock/Syda Productions p47(bc), Shutterstock/whiteMocca p94-95(background), Shutterstock/Yevgenij_D p82-83(background); **Sleep Cycle** p37(c); **Spring Moves** p37(tc); **SWNS** p108(cr); **The Michael C. Rockefeller Memorial Collection**, Bequest of Nelson A. Rockefeller, 1979 p60(B); **Waterlogged** p36(icon br); **Wearefamilyfoundation.org** p51(tr); **Wellcome Collection**/ University College London/Ingrid Lekk and Steve Wilson p48(2); **www.tobiasfraenzel.com** p59(cr).

Video footage and stills supplied by:
BBC Studios Ltd pp49, 61; Digeo Productions pp85, 97; DLA pp25, 73; MTJ pp19, 31, 43, 55, 67, 79, 91, 103, 122, 123, 124; Maia Films pp22, 34, 46, 58, 70, 82, 94, 106

The authors and publishers are grateful for permission to reprint the following copyright material:
p41: Watson NF, Martin JL, Wise MS, Carden KA, Kirsch DB, Kristo DA, Malhotra RK, Olson EJ, Ramar K, Rosen IM, Rowley JA, Weaver TE, Chervin RD. 'Delaying middle school and high school start times promotes student health and performance: an American Academy of Sleep Medicine position statement.' J Clin Sleep Med. 2017;13(4):623–625 p74: HOMESCHOOLING TEEN MAGAZINE © 2016

Additional sources:
Data from British Deaf Association, https://bda.org.uk/
Data from British Museum, https://www.britishmuseum.org/PDF/Chinese_language
Data from Laville, S. and Taylor, M. (28th June 2017) 'A million bottles a minute: world's plastic binge "as dangerous as climate change"', the Guardian
Statistic from Almanza, A., '14 Mind-Blowing Facts About Selfies', Reader's Digest
Statistic from JiWire (June 2012) 'JiWire Mobile Audience Insights Report Q2 2012'
Statistic from Beaton, M., Cortesi, S., Duggan, M., Gasser, U., Lenhart, A., Madden, M. and Smith, A. (21st May 2013) 'Teens, Social Media, and Privacy', Pew Research Centre, pewresearch.org
Macmillan Dictionary, macmillandictionary.com/dictionary/british/fake-news
Data from Helliwell, J., Layard, R. and Sachs, J. (2018) World Happiness Report 2018, New York: Sustainable Development Solutions Network
Bodkin, Henry (13th October 2017) 'Blueberries boost children's brainpower, study finds', The Telegraph Media Group Limited
Data from Northumbria University website (29th April 2016) 'Herbs that can boost your mood and memory'
Hidre´ le´y (November 2018) 'Small Cafe In Toronto Launches Twitter Campaign To Get Ryan Gosling To Visit It, And He Actually Does', boredpanda.com

These materials may contain links for third party websites. We have no control over, and are not responsible for, the contents of such third party websites. Please use care when accessing them.

The inclusion of any specific companies, commercial products, trade names or otherwise does not constitute or imply its endorsement or recommendation by Macmillan Education Limited.

Printed and bound in Poland by CGS

2026 2025 2024 2023 2022
19 18 17 16 15 14 13 12 11 10